Designing Academic Program Reviews

Richard F. Wilson, *Editor*

NEW DIRECTIONS FOR HIGHER EDUCATION

MARTIN KRAMER, *Editor-in-Chief*

Number 37, March 1982

Paperback sourcebooks in
The Jossey-Bass Higher Education Series

Jossey-Bass Inc., Publishers
San Francisco • Washington • London

Designing Academic Program Reviews
Volume X, Number 1, March 1982
Richard F. Wilson, *Editor*

New Directions for Higher Education Series
Martin Kramer, *Editor-in-Chief*

New Directions for Higher Education (publication number USPS 990-880) is published quarterly by Jossey-Bass Inc., Publishers. *New Directions* is numbered sequentially—please order extra copies by sequential number. The volume and issue numbers above are included for the convenience of libraries. Second-class postage rates paid at San Francisco, California, and at additional mailing offices.

Correspondence:
Subscriptions, single-issue orders, change of address notices, undelivered copies, and other correspondence should be sent to *New Directions* Subscriptions, Jossey-Bass Inc., Publishers, 433 California Street, San Francisco, California 94104.

Editorial correspondence should be sent to the Consulting Editor, Martin Kramer, 2807 Shasta Road, Berkeley, California 94708.

Library of Congress Catalogue Card Number LC 81-48479

International Standard Serial Number ISSN 0271-0560

International Standard Book Number ISBN 87589-895-5

Cover art by Willi Baum

Manufactured in the United States of America

Ordering Information

The paperback sourcebooks listed below are published quarterly and can be ordered either by subscription or as single copies.

Subscriptions cost $35.00 per year for institutions, agencies, and libraries. Individuals can subscribe at the special rate of $21.00 per year *if payment is by personal check.* (Note that the full rate of $35.00 applies if payment is by institutional check, even if the subscription is designated for an individual.) Standing orders are accepted.

Single copies are available at $7.95 when payment accompanies order, and *all single-copy orders under $25.00 must include payment.* (California, Washington, D.C., New Jersey, and New York residents please include appropriate sales tax.) For billed orders, cost per copy is $7.95 plus postage and handling. (Prices subject to change without notice.)

To ensure correct and prompt delivery, all orders must give either the *name of an individual* or an *official purchase order number.* Please submit your order as follows:

Subscriptions: specify series and subscription year.
Single Copies: specify sourcebook code and issue number (such as, HE8).

Mail orders for United States and Possessions, Latin America, Canada, Japan, Australia, and New Zealand to:
Jossey-Bass Inc., Publishers
433 California Street
San Francisco, California 94104

Mail orders for all other parts of the world to:
Jossey-Bass Limited
28 Banner Street
London EC1Y 8QE

New Directions for Higher Education Series
Martin Kramer, *Editor-in-Chief*

HE1 *Facilitating Faculty Development,* Mervin Freedman
HE2 *Strategies for Budgeting,* George Kaludis
HE3 *Services for Students,* Joseph Katz
HE4 *Evaluating Learning and Teaching,* Robert Pace
HE5 *Encountering the Unionized University,* Jack Schuster
HE6 *Implementing Field Experience Education,* John Duley
HE7 *Avoiding Conflict in Faculty Personnel Practices,* Richard Peairs
HE8 *Improving Statewide Planning,* James Wattenbarger, Louis Bender
HE9 *Planning the Future of the Undergraduate College,* Donald Trites
HE10 *Individualizing Education by Learning Contracts,* Neal Berte
HE11 *Meeting Women's New Educational Needs,* Clare Rose
HE12 *Strategies for Significant Survival,* Clifford Stewart, Thomas Harvey
HE13 *Promoting Consumer Protection for Students,* Joan Stark
HE14 *Expanding Recurrent and Nonformal Education,* David Harman

HE15 *A Comprehensive Approach to Institutional Development,* William Bergquist, William Shoemaker
HE16 *Improving Educational Outcomes,* Oscar Lenning
HE17 *Renewing and Evaluating Teaching,* John Centra
HE18 *Redefining Service, Research, and Teaching,* Warren Martin
HE19 *Managing Turbulence and Change,* John Millett
HE20 *Increasing Basic Skills by Developmental Studies,* John Roueche
HE21 *Marketing Higher Education,* David W. Barton, Jr.
HE22 *Developing and Evaluating Administrative Leadership,* Charles F. Fisher
HE23 *Admitting and Assisting Students after* Bakke, Alexander W. Astin, Bruce Fuller, Kenneth C. Green
HE24 *Institutional Renewal Through the Improvement of Teaching,* Jerry G. Gaff
HE25 *Assuring Access for the Handicapped,* Martha Ross Redden
HE26 *Assessing Financial Health,* Carol Frances, Sharon L. Coldren
HE27 *Building Bridges to the Public,* Louis T. Benezet, Frances W. Magnusson
HE28 *Preparing for the New Decade,* Larry W. Jones, Franz A. Nowotny
HE29 *Educating Learners of All Ages,* Elinor Greenberg, Kathleen M. O'Donnell, William Bergquist
HE30 *Managing Facilities More Effectively,* Harvey H. Kaiser
HE31 *Rethinking College Responsibilities for Values,* Mary Louise McBee
HE32 *Resolving Conflict in Higher Education,* Jane E. McCarthy
HE33 *Professional Ethics in University Administration,* Ronald H. Stein, M. Carlota Baca
HE34 *New Approaches to Energy Conservation,* Sidney G. Tickton
HE35 *Management Science Applications to Academic Administration,* James A. Wilson
HE36 *Academic Leaders as Managers,* Robert H. Atwell, Madeleine F. Green

Contents

Editor's Notes

It is no small secret that program evaluation is a growth industry in higher education. This growth has been precipitated by a number of interrelated factors, including resource limitations, concerns about maintaining historic strengths and capitalizing on new opportunities, and increased demands for accountability. The response to these new realities has been to establish program evaluation initiatives at every organizational level—department, school, college, campus, system, state, regional, and federal. As with any industry where dynamic growth occurs, it is useful to reflect periodically on what progress has been made and what challenges remain. This sourcebook addresses these two concerns.

In 1979 several of us at the University of Illinois at Urbana-Champaign decided that conceptual and practical knowledge about program evaluation in higher education was expanding rapidly, but avenues for disseminating this information to evaluators were limited. For this reason two national conferences were held, one in 1980 and one in 1981, on the subject of planning and conducting program evaluations and reviews in higher education. This sourcebook contains modified versions of selected presentations at these conferences. The sourcebook, like the conferences, focuses primarily on the evaluation of academic programs. No attempt is made to cover the entire range of activities undertaken under the general rubric of evaluation in higher education. The authors address themselves largely to systematic, rather than ad hoc, procedures, and most of the topics have a campus-level focus. Also, although a university frame of reference is implicit in the treatment of some topics, the principles and concepts presented are applicable to all evaluation settings. The sourcebook is organized around evaluation strategies (Chapters One and Two), evaluation issues (Chapters Three, Four, and Five), evaluation constituencies (Chapters Six and Seven), administrator evaluations (Chapter Eight), and a concluding statement on challenges for the future.

In the first chapter, Ernest R. House describes four evaluation strategies that have received considerable attention and use in recent years; he critiques these strategies in terms of fairness and contribution to program legitimation. The four strategies—system analysis, behavioral, professional review, and case study—each make special contributions and have limitations that should be understood by those engaging in program evaluation. This overview is followed by Hugh G. Petrie's analysis of higher educational institutions as adaptive organizations requiring an adaptive program evaluation process. His central point is that institutions and program evaluation processes interact with each other, and a systemic view of these interactions can help reduce conflict and ensure positive results.

As part of these two discussions of alternative evaluation strategies, several issues are identified that receive specific attention in subsequent chapters. Chapter Three contains a thorough examination of the philosophical and practical implications of value conflicts in higher education and, by extension, in program evaluation. Paul L. Dressel's objective in this chapter is to alert evaluators to the futility of striving for value-free assessments and to encourage more explicit recognition of the values implicit in evaluation processes and results.

This value orientation is intimately tied to Melvin D. George's discussion on assessing program quality in Chapter Four. Numerous measures have been suggested to aid in the struggle to assess quality, and each reflects a slightly different value perspective. George recommends multiple measures that relate to resources, processes, and products. Examples are provided along with several cautions about the nature of evaluative judgments and the role of both quantitative and qualitative measures.

It is frequently asserted that evaluation systems would be unnecessary if administrators were doing their jobs. This contention assumes that the information system available to administrators is satisfactory for evaluation purposes. In Chapter Five Larry A. Braskamp identifies the principles that undergird a good management information system and then contrasts these principles with those on which an evaluation system should be based. Five principles are identified and are used in assessing the actual program evaluation processes at the University of Nebraska at Lincoln and the University of Illinois at Urbana-Champaign.

The next two chapters draw attention to evaluative constituencies, both internal and external. In Chapter Six, H. Richard Smock presents an argument for giving special attention to the internal human network structure that surrounds and supports evaluative activities within an institution. Smock contends that this network is critical to use of results and is most easily engaged when the evaluation process is responsible in nature.

One important external constituency for most institutions is the state coordinating or governing board. The review of existing programs by these boards has increased dramatically over the past ten years, and, in a growing number of states, such reviews implicate private as well as public institutions. Robert A. Wallhaus examines alternatives in state-level program reviews in light of six key decisions. Institutional and state board perspectives are summarized, and the consequences of specific actions are identified.

Many of the same conditions leading to increased interest in program evaluation in higher education have recently spawned a new activity—administrator evaluation. Experience in this area is limited on most campuses, and there is an even greater paucity of scholarly articles on the topic. In Chapter Eight, Donald P. Hoyt identifies uniqueness, context, fairness, credibility, and validity as important principles that must form the basis for administrator evaluation systems, and he specifies typical responsibilities to assess in evaluating administrative performance. Attention also is given to the way contextual factors can facilitate or impede performance and to key considerations in collecting evaluative information. Hoyt concludes his chapter with five specific recommendations for those undertaking administrator evaluations.

The final chapter explores four major challenges for evaluators in higher education. These challenges include: evaluation of cross-disciplinary issues, refinement of conceptions about and measures of quality, evaluation of nonacademic units, and assessing evaluations. For those interested in exploring evaluation literature further, a topical bibliography is provided.

Richard F. Wilson
Editor

Richard F. Wilson is assistant vice-chancellor for academic affairs and assistant professor of higher education at the University of Illinois at Urbana-Champaign.

There are several fundamentally different approaches to evaluation, but all require that the evaluation be perceived as being fair.

Alternative Evaluation Strategies in Higher Education

Ernest R. House

Why is there so much formal evaluation in places where there used to be so little? Universities have always evaluated professors for promotion and tenure, and public schools have long evaluated teachers for retention and even engaged in some program evaluation. Over the past fifteen years, however, the evaluation of educational programs has reached such a flood tide that it now laps at the walls of almost all universities.

There are several answers to this question, none of them totally satisfying. One is that evaluation enhances rational decision making, but there was decision making before, and presumably it was rational without formal program evaluations. A second answer is that funds have decreased, and certainly many evaluation systems have been spawned by attempts to reduce college budgets. Again, however, cutbacks existed long before the creation of formal evaluation systems. Another major impetus for formal evaluation of educational programs came in 1965 when Senator Robert Kennedy attached an evaluation rider to the Elementary and Secondary Education Act, which provided several billions in new monies to the public schools, particularly funds for educating disadvantaged children. Perhaps the exact weighing of causes for the rise of evaluation must await the historians.

I would like to add another possible cause to the list, however, one which supplements rather than supplants the others. That addition is the

R. Wilson (Ed.). *New Directions for Higher Education: Designing Academic Program Reviews,* no. 37.
San Francisco: Jossey-Bass, March 1982.

necessity of *legitimating* the programs and actions that are taken. I take the notion of "legitimate" here to mean not to excuse or to give false evidence, but rather to justify. That is, evaluation places the program or the administrative decision within a larger context, and its place within this larger context justifies or provides legitimacy.

Evaluation may be used for making specific decisions; if it is not, it may be used to demonstrate that the program or action is as it should be. Evaluation theorists have been saying that evaluation serves decision making, and so it does often. But if it serves no particular decision, that does not mean the evaluation is worthless.

Much evaluation places the program or policy evaluated within a larger setting that seems to justify it. For example, a state board of higher education may review all classics programs within its jurisdiction and declare that the programs as constituted are fine. No direct action results, no decision is taken. Yet the classics programs are legitimated. They may not be *properly* placed within a larger framework or judged in relation to the right framework; the state board may be mistaken about the classics programs. However, some such justification through evaluation may be necessary.

This legitimation function of evaluation is greatly neglected. Much evaluation serves such an intangible purpose. The most important fact about a university evaluation plan may be that the university has one and that it is going about its business in a demonstrably deliberate and responsible manner. The actual structure of the evaluation system may be less important.

What this implies about a society that needs so much legitimation I leave untouched, other than to suggest that in certain arenas, particularly in public arenas, much legitimation is indeed necessary. One must publicly justify what one is doing. Without such explanation, it is difficult to account for the enormous increase in the funding of evaluation at a time when other spending is curtailed. It is useful to keep legitimation in mind when examining different evaluation approaches.

Systems Analysis

There are at least eight different approaches to evaluation, and I would like to discuss four of them—systems analysis, behavioral objectives, professional, and case study approaches (House, 1980). The systems analysis approach, favored by officials in the Washington bureaucracies, consists of defining a few measures (such as test scores or gross national product) as the appropriate outcome measures for the programs, then relating differences in programs to variations in the outcome measures (Rossi and others, 1979). For example, one may believe that literacy is the main function of primary education and hence that elementary school students should score well on standardized tests of basic skills. This may be assumed in spite of whatever goals primary teachers say they are pursuing, and one might judge the elementary school as a failure if its students emerge illiterate.

Or again one might reason that a purpose of programs in higher education is to maintain some minimum level of efficiency. A state board might collect and compare costs per student across various institutions and programs. Costs that are unusually high might be singled out for closer examination. For the most part, the outcome measures would be quantitative indicators, and these outcome measures, whatever they are, would be related to the programs via statistical analyses. In some circumstances, one might conduct an experiment and compare the results to other programs. The Follow Through evaluation, the largest educational evaluation ever conducted in the United States, compared more than twenty programs for disadvantaged youth in grades K–3.

Typical questions for a systems analysis evaluation include, "Are the expected program effects achieved?" "Can the program effects be achieved more efficiently?" and "What are the most efficient programs?" One might expect that a Comprehensive Employment and Training Act (CETA) program will result in a lower unemployment rate for the trainees, whatever else it accomplishes. There is a sense in which it does not matter if the teachers want to build character. The bottom line for systems analysts would be, "Did it decrease unemployment?"

The systems analysis approach assumes a consensus on goals or at least one overriding goal; the problem is to relate the outcome measures to the program. For this purpose, good experimental design is necessary; quantitative research methodology is used extensively. This approach also assumes that the evaluation is undertaken for the purposes of management. In one rendition of this approach (Rossi, Freeman, and Wright, 1979), the key questions posed for all programs are these: (1) Is the intervention reaching the target population? (2) Is it being implemented in the ways specified? (3) Is it effective? (4) How much does it cost? (5) What are its costs relative to its effectiveness?

From these questions it is clear that the evaluators perceive the programs as lying within a particular framework of government reform and that all programs are expected to meet these criteria of government effectiveness. In this conception the evaluator helps the government official by reporting on these particular criteria so that the official may take action. It is not surprising that this approach has gained strong federal government support.

The systems analyst is also very much concerned about the replicability of the evaluation, that is, whether the evaluation results would be unchanged after examination by another group of evaluators. Great weight is placed on reliability of evidence by the use of quantitative social science techniques. The systems analysis approach aspires to being scientific. Other types of evaluations are disparaged as being unscientific. Hence, the authority claimed by systems analysis is that of science in the service of the government.

The difficulty with the systems analysis approach is that educational programs seldom lend themselves to being measured by a few simple quantitative outcomes. Test scores often do not capture the essence of most programs, and cost benefit ratios leave too much unsaid. The evaluation is often based on a few available measures that have no credibility, particularly for the people in the program being assessed. Complex, multiple, even conflicting goals are standard in education, and maximizing one outcome often distorts others. In elementary education, for example, one wants literacy and character-building and pleasure in learning, but these goals often conflict. Furthermore, the quantitative techniques used for analysis are sometimes deceptive. They are less sturdy and reliable that one might imagine. Replication is not the same as objectivity, and a highly reliable measure might be invalid as an indicator of program quality.

There are times and places in which program outcomes can be approximated by a few quantitative outcome measures, and these are the appropriate situations in which to use the systems analysis approach. Generally, one must be careful not to confuse the quantitative model with reality or to confuse test scores or numbers of students with the quality of the program. These are only useful indicators of the judgment one is after, but quantitative models often beguile one into thinking otherwise. The strength of the systems analysis approach is that people are impressed with numbers that appear to be objective. Nothing else carries the same weight, even when the numbers are wrong. Numbers are persuasive and decisive and carry the authority of science in a way that no other evaluation result does.

Behavioral Objectives

The behavioral objectives approach to evaluation, a familiar one, specifies a set of objectives for the program then sees whether the objectives have been achieved. Some people insist that the objectives themselves must be framed in behavioral terms. That is, the statement of objectives should contain observable, measurable behaviors that will count as achievement of the goal. For example, educational objectives should contain phrases specifying exact behaviors of the student. Or, at a more general level, the program objective is to graduate a particular percentage of the students enrolled, subject to certain constraints.

Requests for specifying goals and objectives, particularly in grant proposals, have become standard. The difference between the systems analysis and behavioral objectives approaches lies in the outcome. The systems analysts know what the outcomes of the program should be, regardless of particular program goals. For example, the bottom line for the economy is gross national product or the bottom line for a commercial company is profit, and the program is so judged, regardless of what the program personnel may think. On the other hand, the behavioral objectives approach allows the program personnel to specify particular objectives on which the program will be judged (Popham, 1975).

In the Follow Through evaluation mentioned earlier, more than twenty early childhood programs were compared on only four measures; the primary measure was a standardized achievement test. To be judged successful, a program would have to present high scores on the test for its clients. Although a systems analysis evaluation was used, these twenty programs had hundreds of specified objectives, and these objectives differed dramatically one from the other. If the Follow Through evaluators had chosen the objectives approach to evaluation, they would have had to take account somehow of these various objectives.

The Follow Through personnel strongly objected to the disregard of their particular objectives; people in a program generally expect attention to their unique aspects and aspirations. Certainly, higher education program personnel advance objectives that they deem essential and unique. People often object to the application of nonspecific measures such as the percentage of graduates employed. Credibility is achieved by responding to the specified objectives of the program itself.

Yet, all is not well with the objective approach to evaluation either. Who defines the objectives? Is it possible to define specific behaviors for all the desired outcomes? (One project attempting to define objectives for the high school exhausted itself after specifying 20,000.) Can some kinds of important objectives not be specified at all? How can all these objectives be measured and balanced against one another? In actual practice objectives are often arbitrarily chosen. The lists of program objectives are seldom exhaustive, and as a practical matter only a few of the many objectives can be measured. So an objectives-based evaluation often has an arbitrary quality about it, because it is necessarily based on only a few of the program objectives.

Both the systems analysis and behavioral objectives approaches to evaluation assume rational decision making, but the notions of rationality differ somewhat. The systems analysis approach specifies an outcome measure and tries to determine which alternative maximizes the outcomes. The decision is envisioned as a choice among alternatives, such as two different programs or course of action. The rational choice is to choose the alternative that maximizes one's outcomes or that minimizes one's costs. This notion of rationality, common in economics, emphasizes the decision maker's ability to engage in such abstract calculations and to construe the decision in such a simplified manner. In a sense, the systems analysis approach to evaluation is appropriate to the degree that the problem can be conceived in such terms.

The behavioral objectives approach to evaluation lessens the calculation demands somewhat. One has some objectives and sees whether one has achieved these objectives. Rationality is construed as the congruence between one's goals and outcomes, a lesser demand. One sees whether one is moving in the right direction rather than being assured that one has maximized potential. The behavioral objectives approach is derived from task analysis. Its rationality is to reduce the overall behavior into smaller steps that are more manageable, just as one does on an assembly line—a technological or engineering approach.

Hence, the world in which legitimation occurs is a technological world, a world in which tasks are related to secondary tasks, via objectives, and to higher objectives; all of these tasks are finally subsumed within the overall goals and purposes of the organization itself. Again, this way of thinking has a powerful hold on the American imagination, and some people believe that when every objective is related to every other, the program is properly arranged.

Professional Review

Both the systems analysis and behavioral objectives approaches presume to be scientific. They base part of their claim to authority on the methods that they employ. Presumably, these methods—derived from the social sciences—produce objective information through psychometric measurement, rigorous experimental design, statistical methods of relating data, and quantitative methods of inquiry in general. Certain methods of investigation are assumed to ensure objectivity and truth.

In contrast to the scientific approaches, one might take a rather different tack. One might evaluate programs through what I would call humanistic approaches, based upon experience rather than method. The experience might be acquired in different ways and be expressed in different forms but the evaluation proceeds from accumulated experience. I will discuss two such approaches: professional review and case study.

Professional review in higher education is exemplified by the visits of accreditation teams associated with a particular specialty. The accreditation team is selected from outside experts, and these people review program documents, visit the program sites, and write a report on the program's strengths and weaknesses (National Study of School Evaluation, 1978). The standards they use to make their judgments are based upon their personal experience as professionals within their specialty and upon the experience of the profession as a whole. There are often written codes, rules, and criteria that the visitors are required to employ. Presumably, these codes arise from and are validated by the profession as a whole, although no particular profession would agree with all of them. This approach engages program staff in the evaluation. The staff is asked to prepare material and to appraise their own program. Outside judgments are then compared to those of the staff. So the accreditation visit serves as an opportunity for self-examination, at least in theory.

A recent variation of the professional review approach is the evaluation of departments within a university by professors and administrators from within the university. One example is the Council on Program Evaluation at the University of Illinois. A council of nine professors and four students, chaired by a university administrator, has overseen the first cycle of evaluation of most departments in the university. Formal criteria employed in the evaluation include quality of instruction, quality of research, quality of service, importance to the campus, value to the society, and future prospects of the specialty. Of course, how these criteria are implemented is critical.

The two methods of data collection in the first cycle were special task groups appointed to directly examine a department and a self-report set of forms and questionnaires filled out by the department. In both cases the collected information was brought back to the council, which prepared an evaluative report for the department and for the general public.

The primary advantage of these professional review approaches is that they are acceptable to the professionals themselves (although sometimes the faculty do not accept the judgments of on-campus colleagues from other disciplines). Professionals are judging professionals. Their main weakness is that the reviews are often regarded with suspicion by the general public, which sometimes believes that professionals do not evaluate themselves rigorously. For example, many people believe that doctors will not testify against doctors. The public suspects that the evaluations are self-serving and "without teeth."

Another problem is that the approach requires a great deal of work on the part of the professionals. Preparing for an accreditation visit is laborious for those visited, and it does not contribute directly to their professional lives. In the case of the Council on Program Evaluation, professors were reluctant to serve on an investigating task group more than once, primarily because of the demand on their time. Similarly, preparation of the appropriate evaluation forms by the departments was immensely time consuming.

Still, there are insights resulting from one professional judging another professional that are unavailable elsewhere. No one knows better or can come closer to a professional program than another professional. In spite of public suspicions, professional review remains a viable and useful approach. Professional review legitimates a program within the world of relevant professionals, a world of arcane and specialized knowledge and authority.

Case Study

Case study or case history, the final evaluation approach involves an evaluator coming into a program and constructing a narrative, a story as it were, of what the program is all about. The case is usually constructed by interviewing faculty members, students, and administrators about the program. Often the story of the program is told in the words of the participants. Whereas in the professional review approach, one relies upon the experience of professionals, here one relies upon the experience of the program's participants. Authenticity is gained through direct contact.

The primary question asked is, "What does the program look like to various people who are familiar with it?" The methods employed can be anthropological or even journalistic (Stake, 1978). So far, the approach has been employed in higher education mainly in the smaller colleges that lend themselves to an overall impressionistic summary. There is no reason, however, why the case approach cannot be employed with larger universities and the departments and programs within them.

In a case study, one ends up with a document which is highly readable even to nonspecialists. If well done, it incorporates the perceptions of those who are most familiar with the program, both the proponents and detractors. It can serve as a springboard for discussion and a prelude to future decisions about the program. It incorporates a wide range of information not available to most other approaches because almost anything the evaluator encounters may be included.

A major premise of the case approach, I believe, is that one must know what has happened and is happening to the program to know its prospects. Every program, like every person, is bound to its past. Furthermore, to understand the program truly, one must see it through the eyes of its participants, for it has significance and meaning to them that only they understand. This meaning is decipherable only through their words, even if one disagrees with the meaning which they ascribe to it. The idea to which the case worker aspires is that the evaluation be recognizable and acceptable to the participants themselves as well as to an outside audience. So its major strength is its aspiration for authenticity.

Its major weakness is its subjectivity. How does the reader know how much of the evaluation is the program and how much is the evaluator? Where does the evaluator obtain the standards for the evaluation and how does he or she employ them? Is not a good portion of the case mainly the evaluator's opinion? How does one find an evaluator with the requisite writing skills, balance, and judgment to trust with a portrayal of the program? When one moves away from ordained method, much legitimacy resides with the personal experience of the evaluator. These are some of the problems of the case study approach to evaluation.

Fairness

As a final topic, let me turn to an issue that concerns not the legitimacy of programs but rather the legitimacy of evaluation itself—the issue of fairness, without which no evaluation can be perceived as legitimate.

Several years ago I was appointed as a faculty member to the Council on Program Evaluation (COPE). At the first meeting I attended, the council was discussing a recommendation to abolish the College of Communications. The college consisted of the departments of journalism, advertising, and radio-television. According to this recommendation, journalism and advertising would be moved into other colleges, and radio-television would be disbanded altogether, along with the administration. The College of Communications would cease to exist as a unit.

I was astounded, first, because of the radicalness of the action and, second, because of the history of the evaluations that had preceded the review of the College of Communications. About twenty departments had been evaluated previously, and although several had been found wanting, none had been penalized in any significant way. Suddenly, without warning, the College of Communications was to be pulled out of the line and shot in the head. Two of the departments—journalism and advertising—had received quite favorable evaluations. Only radio-television had received a bad evaluation. Yet the recommendation proposed was to abolish the college.

The recommendation was sent to the chancellor's office where it became public. During the fall and winter, the College of Communications conducted a strong campaign through its graduates, who staffed radio, television, and journalism posts in the Chicago and national media. The battle was one-sided. At winter registration 10,000 student signatures were collected protesting the abolition of the college. Not since coed dorms were established, said the chancellor, had there been so much mail from the public. Throughout this fierce activity, the main rallying point against the evaluation was not so much the content of the report as the idea that the college had been unfairly treated.

In the spring the chancellor called the council in and said, "I don't know about the educational merits of your recommendation, but the political costs are too high to implement it." The college was retained, although the radio and television department was overhauled drastically. Serious questions were raised about the council activities, and the next year the faculty senate appointed a committee to evaluate the COPE operation itself. The evaluators were suspect.

The moral of this story concerns the notion of fairness. For an evaluation system to operate, it must be perceived as being fair. Fairness is based upon the expectations that one has about the situation in question. The College of Communications assumed that nothing drastic would happen to it as a result of the COPE evaluation since nothing had happened to previous departments. The college received no advance warning and suddenly it was subjected to rather arbitrary action. In no sense was the college treated equally with other departments. The wrong that it received was a moral wrong, and it reacted passionately against it, as people do with moral outrages. The council should have made it clear that abolishment was a possible result before the evaluation.

Generally, judgments of fairness proceed from an understanding or agreement that one has with other people. If one does certain things, then other people are expected to do certain things in return. Often the understanding is tacit rather than explicit. It may be based on past actions rather than on a detailed, explicit, written agreement. Such was the case with COPE and the

College of Communications. If one party does its part according to the understanding and the other party does not, the other party's behavior is considered to be unfair. Fairness is a quality that evaluations absolutely must possess if they are to be perceived as legitimate, regardless of what approach to evaluation is employed.

To facilitate fairness, any evaluation system should have certain features:

- It should have an explicated set of procedures
- These procedures should be publicly known
- These procedures and rules should be consistently applied (Consistency, after all, is a cornerstone of justice)
- There should be provisions for confidentiality of information, and these should be understood by all at the beginning
- There should be restrictions on the use of informal information, that is, considerations not included in the evaluation reports
- There should be avenues for recourse and redress
- Strong administrative support is necessary if these procedures are to be carried out equally with all parties, even those who are especially influential.

Over the long run, an evaluation system may or may not be useful, but it must be fair. Otherwise, it is not worth retaining. The world of legitimation here is the moral one, the one that regulates relationships among people.

In summary, the evaluations legitimize the programs and the evaluations themselves are legitimized by being seen as being fair. The programs are perceived as being legitimate because they have been properly scrutinized. They have been put to the test. The evaluation is considered legitimate because the proper procedures have been followed, whatever these procedures may be. Note that legitimacy is a political notion. That is, one's interests must be properly and procedurally protected. Our evaluations, like our elections, must be fair.

All in all, what approach does one employ? This is a difficult decision, a bit like the choice of a spouse. Success is not guaranteed. Much depends upon the audience for the evaluation, the circumstances, and the resources available. Different audiences accept different kinds of evidence as important. My favorite approach is the case study, but state legislators are unlikely to be impressed with this kind of evidence or even take the time to read it. They usually like numbers, even though they may not understand them. University professionals are quite likely to favor the professional review approach, since faculty participation is so important in academia. All methods have special strengths and weaknesses. All can be improved upon. As a practical matter, evaluators should explore with their primary audiences the type of evaluation both parties find acceptable. This agreement or understanding can then serve as the basis of the evaluation.

References

House, E. R. *Evaluating with Validity.* Beverly Hills, Calif.: Sage, 1980.

National Study of School Evaluation. *Evaluative Criteria.* Arlington, Va.: National Study of School Evaluation, 1978.

Popham, W. J. *Educational Evaluation.* Englewood Cliffs, N.J.: Prentice-Hall, 1975.

Rossi, P. H., Freeman, H. E., and Wright, S. R. *Evaluation: A Systematic Approach.* Beverly Hills, Calif.: Sage, 1979.

Stake, R. E. "The Case Study Method in Social Inquiry." *Educational Researcher,* 1978, *7* (2), 5–8.

Ernest R. House is professor of administration, higher, and continuing education in the Center for Instructional Research and Curriculum Evaluation at the University of Illinois at Urbana-Champaign.

If program evaluation is to be integrated into, rather than resisted by, an institution, both the evaluation scheme and the institution must be analyzed as adaptive systems.

Program Evaluation as an Adaptive System

Hugh G. Petrie

There are any number of ways to think about program evaluation. In this chapter I want to think about program evaluation in a systemic way. Notice that I did not say "systematic" way. For my part, I receive little benefit from going down systematic checklists, making certain I have put tab A into slot B, and so on. Nor am I urging a "systems analysis" view of program evaluation. Indeed, any such input-output analysis will be wholly inadequate from the viewpoint of adaptive systems. However, viewing organizations as adaptive systems and seeing certain organizational developments as attempts to change systems can be very useful, indeed. I will explore such a viewpoint here.

One of the constantly recurring complaints in evaluation is that the results of the evaluation all too seldom make a difference. How is it that we can so readily agree upon the desirability of evaluating and so seldom see any practical results of the evaluation? Even in those cases where there is ostensibly a decision, say, to cut a program, the actual implementation may never take place. Evaluators have attempted to dismiss such recurring embarrassments with a variety of excuses. At one extreme, they define "evaluation" so that such lapses are not really their fault. Evaluators only gather information, they say; others must make decisions and implement them. This results in the absurdity of evaluation without value judgments. At the other extreme, evaluators claim that "political" pressures distort the rational results and implica-

R. Wilson (Ed.). *New Directions for Higher Education: Designing Academic Program Reviews,* no. 37. San Francisco: Jossey-Bass, March 1982.

tions of evaluation. This ploy results in the absurdity of evaluations that are designed to produce changes but, nevertheless, have nothing to do with action. And, of course, there are numerous excuses in between.

What I want to suggest is that at least one frequent reason for the oft-noted rupture between evaluation and action is a failure to take a systems view of the situation. The systems view must focus, first, on the organization to be evaluated, and, second, on the proposed program evaluation system. Do the two systems complement or oppose each other? It is a well-known feature of systems in conflict that they effectively cancel each other's action. Thus, care must be taken to understand both the organization and the proposed evaluation program as interactive systems, which will mesh with, rather than oppose, each other if they are appropriately designed and implemented.

Adaptive Systems

Any structure that engages in value-guided action can be usefully considered an adaptive system. Thinking about organizations and program evaluation as adaptive systems will help focus on the design and implementation aspects of a program evaluation system. Adaptive systems theory provides a general model that is applicable across a variety of types of institutions. It focuses on the systemic interactions within program evaluation and across other parts of the institutional ecology. It draws attention to the crucial phases of the system where if anything can go wrong, it will.

What is an adaptive system? Probably the most familiar example is the common household thermostat. Schematically, such a system looks like the one presented in Figure 1. Using the thermostat as an example, the reference signal is the desired temperature, the thermostat setting. For an institution of higher education, the reference signal would be the various goals and purposes that the institution and its units were pursuing, either implicitly or explicitly. In program evaluation the reference signal might be, for example, the criterion of high-quality programs.

The perceptual input is the temperature-sensing device, which senses the ambient temperature of the house and represents it as an appropriate signal. For higher education the perceptual signals involve everything from class sizes, curricula, and degrees to faculty salaries, retention procedures, and morale. In program evaluation, the perceptual input is the way in which information is gathered concerning programs, and the perceptual signals are the data that represent the programs to the evaluating mechanism.

The comparator is the device that compares perceptual signal with reference signal to see if the two match. If they do, nothing is required; if the two signals do not match, the difference is the error signal that drives the output, thereby correcting the error. In the example of the thermostat, the comparator is the thermostat itself. In higher education the comparators are the mechanisms—from top administration to faculty senate, individual faculty, and stu-

Figure 1. Thermostat Analogy

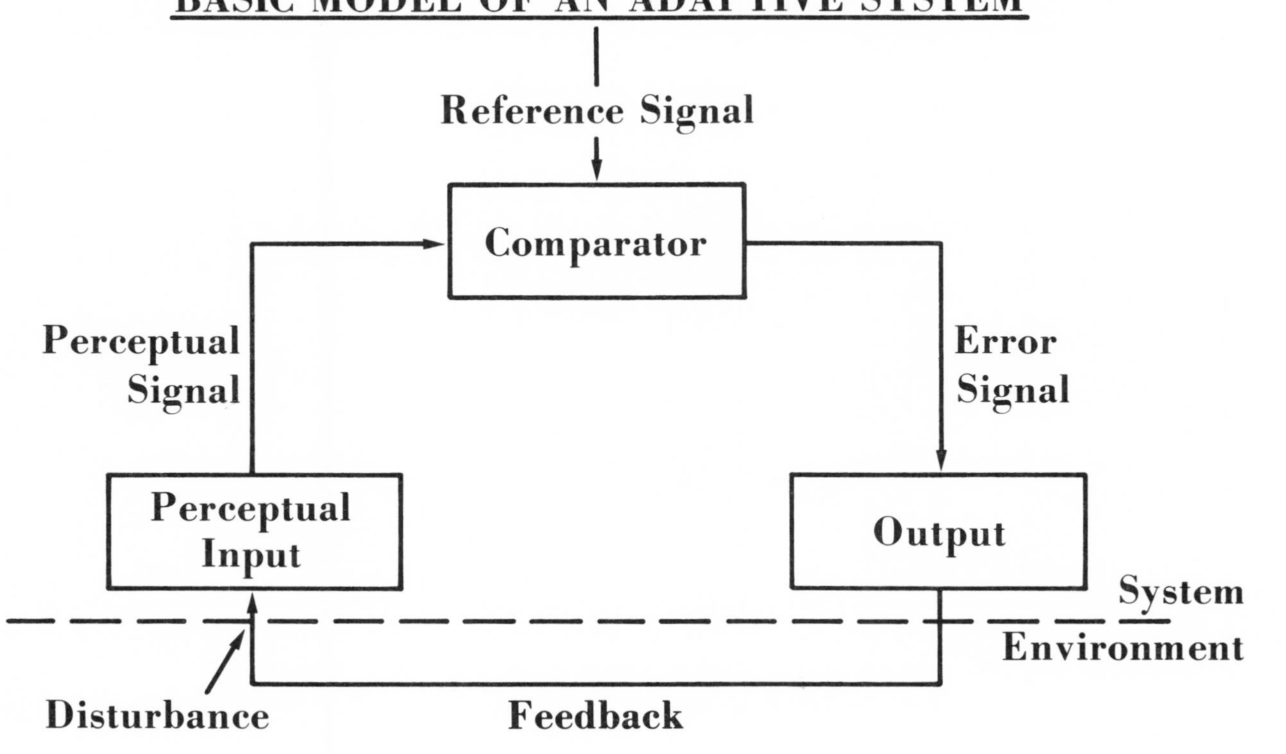

dents—constantly comparing what they experience against what they believe the institution should be. In program evaluation the comparator is the basic mechanism by which the judgments are made of how well the program meets the criteria. In the thermostat the error signal is the electrical impulse to the furnace. In higher education the error signals include student revolts, faculty morale, and calls for curricular revision. In program evaluation, the error signal is the reporting and recommending that issue from the evaluations. Note, too, that adaptive systems have a certain range of tolerance. The error has to be big enough to call for a correction.

The output or effector function is designed to have an effect on the environment. For the thermostat the output is, of course, the furnace, which circulates heat through the environment. For an institution of higher education, the outputs are budgeting decisions, faculty recruitment activities, enrollment targets, and so on. Notice that, unlike a systems analysis view, the outputs are not the usual degrees granted or articles published. Such a conception would be about 90° (25 percent) out of phase. For an adaptive system the output is what changes the environment so that it looks more like what the reference signal wants. Thus, in program evaluation, the effector function is whatever device that actually makes a change—from a board of regents' decision to eliminate a program to a dean's reallocation of funds to strengthen a program.

The feedback through the environment consists of the causal results of the operation of the output function. With the thermostat it is the circulation of the heat through the house. For the institution it may be actual enrollments, degrees granted, research grants obtained, or articles published. In program evaluation it is the effects of the various decisions on the programs being evaluated. These are, of course, complex effects, but for my purposes I will simply assume that these effects operate in a natural way, much as the heated air circulates through a house. If the outputs really do change the environment in the desired way, well and good; if not, then the system is not adequate to control its environment.

Finally, there is what I have called a disturbance affecting the input function. In the case of a thermostat this is usually the heat loss from the house, although it can be as dramatic as an open window next to the thermostat on a cold night. In higher education a disturbance can be anything from a slow deterioration in the quality of a department to a change of leadership or a rapid rise or fall of enrollments. Anything external to the system that can affect the input quantities is a disturbance.

The concept of a disturbance is an important one for the notion of an adaptive system. Adaptive systems maintain the perceptual signal as close to the reference signal as possible. A disturbance changes the input signal, so an adaptive system counteracts disturbances. To put it another way, adaptive systems model the notion of management by exception very well. This feature explains the extreme resistance to certain kinds of change found in most organizations. Change is perceived, often implicitly, as a disturbance to the desired reference signal and so, as with the thermostat, actions are undertaken to remove the disturbance. But, it might be objected, this approach is puzzling in the extreme. How can one call a system that resists changes adaptive? Surely that is a mark of rigidity. There are three parts to the answer. First, we must be absolutely clear as to what is changing—the system or the environment. For an adaptive system, a change in the environment is a disturbance to the system's operation. It needs to change its behavior to resist the disturbance. The system changes its outputs to change the environment back to what it wants; the system thus adapts to a changing environment. A drop in enrollments is followed by behavior to bring the enrollments back to the levels desired—increasing recruiting, adult education, and so on. In an adaptive system all sorts of changes in output occur for the sake of keeping something else unchanged; the perceptual signal matches the reference signal. For normal ranges of disturbance, such operation is highly adaptive.

Second, however, depending on the environment, not all efforts to resist disturbance will prove adaptive. Sometimes the disturbance overwhelms the system's normal range of control. Just as a thermostat on a bitterly cold night in a poorly insulated house will run the furnace continuously without reaching 68°F, so also may some institutions spend their last dollar on a flashy recruiting brochure when the students for that institution no longer exist. In such extremes the "adaptive" system is, of course, no longer adaptive.

Third, in such extreme cases, the environmental disturbances call, not for the ordinary changes in output to resist disturbances, but for changes in the way the system itself operates. We can lower the thermostat setting, put in a more powerful furnace, insulate the house, move to a warmer climate, and so on.

Instituting a program evaluation system may well be viewed by the organization as a disturbance to its operation, and, if so, it will be resisted by the organization. This is especially likely if the evaluation system is being imposed externally as part of an accountability scheme in which accountability means something quite different to the external agency than it does to the institution. I am, of course, not suggesting that external accountability is necessarily inappropriate. I am only saying that no one should be surprised when such pressures are resisted by the organization. Correlatively, if the decision is made to incorporate concerns of external constituencies into the institutional program review process, fundamental changes in the institution may be required.

In what follows, however, I assume that there is no fundamental conflict between the intended purposes of the evaluation system and the organization. The question then becomes one of designing the evaluation system to capitalize on the systemic properties of the existing organization rather than to create disturbance that will be resisted. A well-designed program evaluation system will then monitor and correct disturbances to higher education programs.

This brief overview of program evaluation and higher education conceived as adaptive systems suggests three main groups of questions that should be asked. These questions correspond to the three sub-units of the adaptive system—the comparator, the input functions, and the effector functions. Correspondingly, the questions are: (1) How are criteria formulated and interpreted? This is the comparator question, and it has to do primarily with the processes for determining whether the perceptions one has gathered concerning a program match the criteria for what the program ought to resemble. (2) How is information gathered and represented? This is the input or perceptual question. It concerns the data or indicators used to represent the program, for example, student loans, budgets, research productivity, peer judgments, and degrees granted. (3) How are effects implemented? This is the output or effector question, which involves the sort of "furnace" if any, to which the program evaluation system is connected. That is, to whom recommendations are made and what powers the evaluation system has to demand change. Taken together, these three questions are the primary ones to be asked of any model of an adaptive system.

Consider the more detailed model or program evaluation conceived of as an adaptive system and shown in Figure 2. The following discussion elaborates on the main features of this model.

Purposes and Criteria of Evaluation

Let me begin by introducing a rough distinction among three concepts that are sometimes confused—purposes, criteria, and indicators. *Purposes* are the reasons for doing an evaluation and are explicit in varying degrees. Program improvement is often an explicitly stated purpose of program evaluation. Protection against external interference might be a less explicit purpose in some cases. *Criteria* are the dimensions in terms of which the program is to be judged. Typically these include quality and centrality. *Indicators* are data viewed in light of criteria. For example, a datum of declining enrollments in a given field seen against a criterion of social need would indicate a negative judgment on a program. At the same time declining enrollments seen against a criterion of high-quality instruction might indicate a positive judgment on a program, especially if previous enrollments had resulted in overcrowded classes. That is, the same information can indicate quite different evaluative judgments depending on the criteria used.

I have mixed emotions about explicit evaluative criteria. I suppose one cannot simply ignore them; however, I am thoroughly convinced that they are not a panacea. No one can or should develop criteria to the level of explicitness that the criteria could serve as a checklist for conducting evaluations. The context will always potentially make a difference, and only the people who live in that context will be able to judge what the data indicate in light of the criteria. Nevertheless, the process of developing criteria helps sensitize people to the issues involved and the salient features that they must consider in evaluation,

Figure 2. Model of Program Evaluation

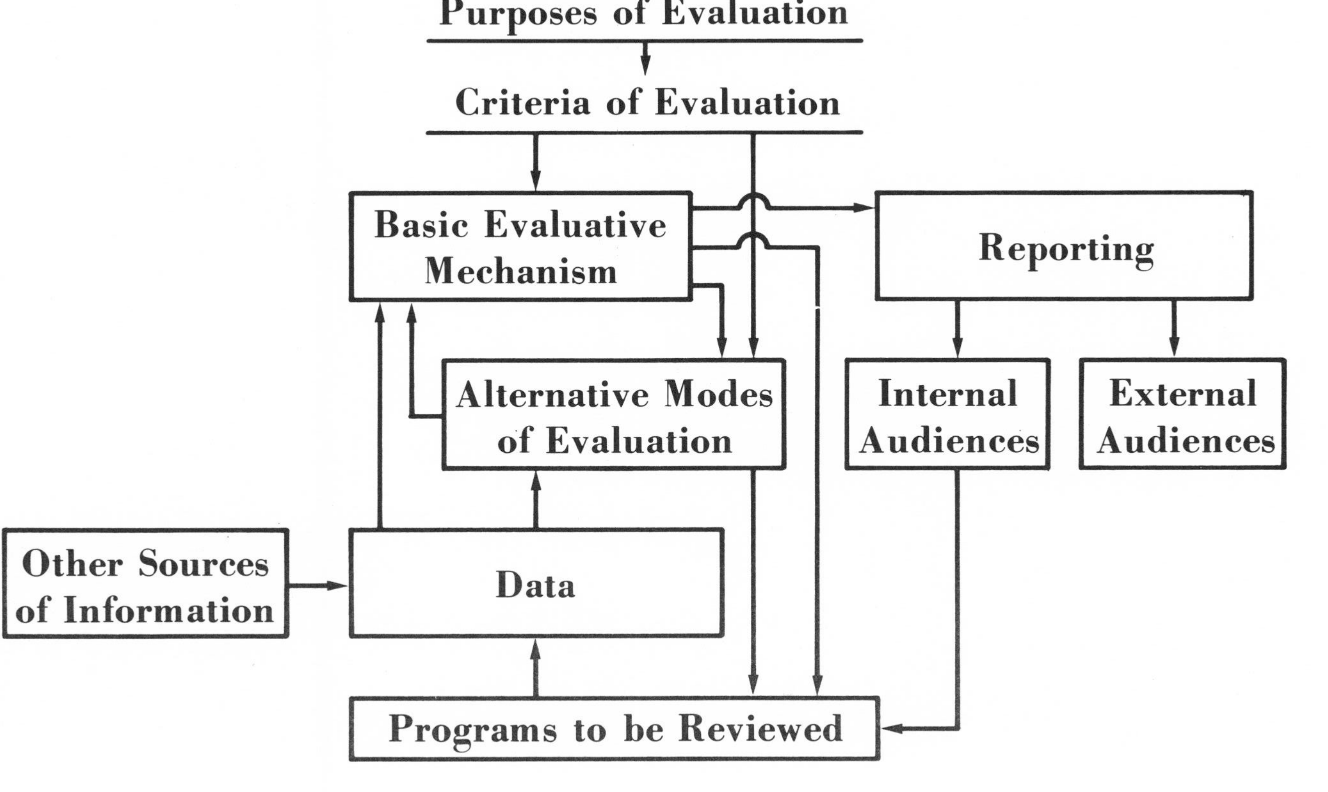

even though the final product will require wise judgment rather than a summary of criteria met and unmet. In short, one should go through a process of developing criteria that encourages widespread institutional participation, but should not allow this stage to dominate the process.

Of far more importance is the necessity for understanding the criteria in light of the purposes of the evaluation. Consider, for example, the State of New York's criteria for the evaluation of doctoral programs—quality and need. Need includes sustaining the expansion and transmission of knowledge in even the most esoteric fields. I submit that the need for esoteric knowledge will look quite different as a criterion if the purpose of the review is program improvement than it will if the purpose is budget reallocation. The point is to make sure that the criteria are congruent with the purposes. If the evaluation is multipurpose, purposes may end up pulling in opposite directions, and one should be explicit that this may happen.

Basic Evaluative Mechanism

Understanding the criteria in light of the purposes brings me to the basic evaluative mechanism. Remember that the basic evaluative mechanism is the comparator in the adaptive systems model, and it makes the fundamental judgments about the value of a program. As I have just indicated, different forms of the basic evaluative mechanism may emphasize different purposes for the evaluation and in turn will tend to apply the "same" criteria differently.

Of course, any number of arrangements are possible. Many are mentioned elsewhere in this sourcebook. The crucial point to remember is that the kind of basic mechanism and the people chosen for it will influence the judgments made. Nowhere is the danger of disturbing the organization by introducing an evaluation system more apparent than in the design of the basic evaluative mechanism. If the basic mechanism holds values opposed to the institutional values, problems will result. For example, a centralized review of costs per credit hour will be viewed as a disturbance on a research campus committed to disciplinary scholarship. Alternatively, a peer review of research quality by well-known scholars in the field will be viewed as a disturbance by a college devoted to undergraduate teaching. On a unionized campus a program evaluation system could easily be viewed as a disturbance by the union, especially if it calls for reductions in force.

Sometimes the basic evaluative mechanism delegates certain evaluations; sometimes supplementary evaluations are required. These alternative modes of evaluation receive direction from both the overall purposes of the evaluation and the basic mechanism. Likewise, they will be given data as well as generate their own and will report to the basic mechanism and to the programs being reviewed. Alternative modes of evaluation thus serve as a kind of subsystem in the overall system.

Data

Perhaps the most important point concerning the data, or perceptual inputs, for a program evaluation system is that the data must be relevant to the purposes and criteria of the evaluation. This is a point made in many of the other chapters, but it can scarcely be overemphasized. For if the data and criteria are incommensurable, the system will be wholly unable to sense whether the program meets the criteria or not. Worse yet, inappropriate data may call forth the use of implicit criteria quite different from those ostensibly guiding the evaluation.

Another major problem, both practical and conceptual, in talking about data for program evaluation is that data necessarily represent programs. It is a truism, but one that evaluators too often overlook, that the data they examine are not the same things as the programs they are to evaluate. The problem is not simply one of abstraction. Of course, one loses information as one abstracts more and more. Departments are concerned with the particulars of their students. The campus is concerned with the enrollment trends in the department, and the boards of higher education are concerned with overall enrollments at the institutions of their state. Each level has lost some detail of information. By collecting gross enrollment statistics, we may also distort what is going on. Can one tell from enrollment data, for example, that a large portion of the drop in history enrollments is due to a drop in the number of students seeking teacher certification in high school social studies? Will one be able to determine that the continued stability in enrollment in economics is due to a vast increase in the percentage of questionably qualified foreign students? Will the state be able to see that although the overall enrollment at a given institution may be stable, there are significant internal pressures with students straining the capacities of the technical high-cost programs and avoiding the low-cost programs?

It is not that gross enrollment data abstracts from these questions; it is rather than such data were never designed to answer them in the first place. Indeed, it is my view that the gross enrollment categories that institutions have used are part of the problem. The recent huge influx of foreign students, especially to expensive private schools, has in part been caused by gross student body counting. The increased recruitment competition among state schools is obvious testimony to the fact that how we represent our programs in terms of the data we collect has enormous impact on what we do. How we keep score determines how we play the game.

Closely allied to the representation problem is *presentation*. Mundane and uninteresting as it may seem, most evaluative mechanisms simply cannot assimilate table after table of numbers. Regardless of how good the design of an evaluation system may be and how carefully the data sources are selected, the basic evaluative mechanism may still flounder. It may flounder because it cannot interpret the data that is being thrown at it. The presentation of the data must be carefully considered as well as what and how much is collected. Indeed, in some instances and for some purposes, a brief narrative case study may be more meaningful and useful than reams of computer printouts.

Another crucial point to appreciate about data is that although they should be limited in amount, they should come from multiple sources. If peer reputation, statistical information, and faculty and student judgments all seem to indicate the same general things, one can be fairly confident of the final conclusions. On the other hand, if the peer judgment is good, but the students and faculty are unhappy, there may be a problem with the leadership of a program. Conversely, if students and faculty are happy, but the faculty is not doing much scholarly work and the peer judgments are poor, perhaps a mediocre unit needs attention. Multiple sources of information help guard against the possibility of being misled.

Let me give a detailed example of the need for multiple sources of evaluation. Both faculty and student surveys of a certain department indicate some dissatisfaction, especially with the unit's leadership. At the same time research support and published scholarship are increasing. The head has also just maneuvered the unit into new and more adequate facilities, and the department now controls a service course in the college that assures both undergraduate enrollments and teaching assistant jobs for graduate students. Upon further investigation, it becomes clear that several years ago the head had been brought in to shake things up and move the department out of the doldrums. The head was succeeding in doing this, although the effects on some faculty and students who preferred the old regime were negative. In short, an indicator, negative by itself, may be part of an overall positive picture. In this case dissatisfaction turned out to be a positive indicator.

A final point should be obvious to anyone even passingly familiar with program evaluation. Information is not free. It has a cost, and careful judgments needs to be made about the benefits of collecting any kind of information versus its cost. I do not believe that the benefits of collecting a given kind of information need to outweigh the cost for each program evaluated. That would be too stringent a requirement. But on the whole, for the system, the benefits should outweigh the costs.

Effects

Finally, let me turn to the effector function of the adaptive systems model of program evaluation. If the thermostat is not hooked up to a furnace, little heat is likely to be generated. The major question to ask of the effects is whether they are leading to the situations denoted by the reference signal. Are they removing disturbances?

Reporting is, of course, one of the basic effects of an evaluation. The questions are, "To whom does one report and in how much detail?" Once more the answer should be guided by the purposes and criteria of the evaluation. There are also the questions of internal versus external audiences, confidentiality, and the level of detail that should be reported.

Clearly if the system is to have resource reallocation as a primary purpose, it must be connected to where resource decisions are made. If one hopes to reallocate resources and then designs a system that reports essentially just on educational quality to the unit being evaluated, one should not be surprised if the evaluation system does nothing.

The problem of meshing the program evaluation system with the organizational system at the level of actually instituting change is one of the longest standing and most perplexing problems in the short history of program evaluation in higher education. Many of the ways in which the evaluation can be seen as a disturbance by the organizational system have already been mentioned. Here I would like to add just one more. Traditional administrators in higher education see themselves as performing program evaluation in the ordinary course of their duties in many ways. To have a structure erected alongside or in place of the traditional one strikes many of them as otiose, if not downright humiliating. At the same time, the traditional structure is the one through which any changes will be made. What better way to strike back at the program evaluation system than to ignore its reports and recommendations? The implication is clear. Department heads, deans, and vice-chancellors must be committed to the program evaluation system and ultimately involved in making it work.

However, one should not underestimate the quite indirect and unplanned effects that the mere existence of an evaluative system will have on programs. Even with careful design some units may well perceive an evaluation system as a disturbance to their mode of operation. They can sometimes be highly imaginative in trying to remove the disturbance. Some units will try to frustrate the evaluation; others will try to preempt it.

Let me give an example of preemption. One of the recommendations of a departmental review was to look at a possible merger with a second department to be reviewed later. When the second unit was reviewed, a merger between the two seemed at least *prima facie* plausible, and so the evaluation group decided to pursue the matter further. The dean of the affected college was asked to meet with the evaluation group for some preliminary discussions, and he was informed of the topics of the discussion in general terms. By the time the meeting took place, the dean had established an internal committee with a slightly broader charge than to consider a merger, but still with more than enough overlap to effectively preempt the campus evaluation. In short, one should not underestimate the response of "We already knew about that and are working on it." At the same time, however, such responses at least indicate that the unit perceives the disturbance as something that it can and should do something about, and thus exemplifies an evaluation system that meshes with the organizational system.

There are other benefits of simply having the evaluation system in place. Some units will take the opportunity of a scheduled campus evaluation to do a thorough and wide-ranging self-study, one that may well go far beyond what the official evaluation would require. Units that do this uniformly report good consequences. Of course, any of these activities could occur without an institutional system of program evaluation, but the system seems to move them to the forefront. Unless the faculty and administrators at an institution are completely incompetent, they will already have a general knowledge of the strengths and weaknesses of their programs. What a properly designed system of evaluation can do is to confirm these suspicions, flesh them out, and engage people's attention in a systematic way in trying to solve the problems.

Of even more importance, however, is the possibility that if the evaluation system meshes properly with the organizational system, it can be of real assistance in two main ways. First, the people involved with the program are bound to become more reflective about their tasks and how well they are performing them during an evaluation, and ultimately the people in the program will be the ones to make any changes. Second, bringing the norms and standards of the whole institution to bear on a given program sometimes has a salutary effect. Even if the unit already recognizes its problems, it may have been just the extra suggestion from outside that is needed to be solving them.

Finally, let me return for a moment to those situations in which the evaluation system intentionally ceates a disturbance beyond the normal range of control of the organizational system. In such cases one must be prepared for conflict. Organizations will resist such changes in what appears to them to be a very adaptive way, but which will appear as unadaptive to outsiders. The only hope for achieving such fundamental changes lies in identifying underlying values and organizing metaphors that allow both the outside evaluators and the institution to see their efforts as part of a new way of making sense of their common predicament. Such philosophical concerns are not usually seen as part of evaluation, but if I am correct, there are occasions in which they must be. These occasions occur when the evaluation system cannot be meshed into the organization system and when the organization must undergo fundamental changes to truly adapt to a changed situation.

One current example may be the somewhat negative evaluation of liberal arts education implicit in society's renewed emphasis on career education and professional training. Since the late 1960s support for general education has been declining while demand for engineering and business training has been increasing. Many regional universities have already become almost totally business and engineering schools. Such fundamental changes may be impossible to reverse. On the other hand, well-established comprehensive universities have tried to resist basic changes in their structure, but the outcome of the struggle is still in doubt. Enormous tensions exist in such institutions between professional programs with high demand and liberal arts colleges with decreased student interest. Reallocation decisions are complicated and have far-reaching consequences. For example, even if some balance is retained, what happens to an institution in which some programs turn away students in the ninetieth percentile of their high school class while other programs admit students from the fiftieth percentile? We seem unable in principle to determine when we are at such critical junctures, except *ex post facto*.

In any event the systems view can help to identify the problems and at least the areas in which we must search for solutions. It may help us to design evaluation systems that mesh with, rather than oppose, our organizational systems. What are the values and goals of the institution? Are these compatible with the goals and values of the program evaluation system? What features of its environment does the institution see? What features does the evaluation system look at? Are these compatible with each other? With the goals of the two systems? What changes can the institution make? What changes can the evaluation system effect? Will these changes affect the situation that the evaluation system is meant to monitor? These are the questions that must be asked of an evaluation system intended to help the institution be truly adaptive.

Hugh G. Petrie is dean of the Faculty of Education Studies at the State University of New York at Buffalo. From 1977 to 1980, he served as associate vice-chancellor for academic affairs and chair of the Council on Program Evaluation at the University of Illinois at Urbana-Champaign.

A plurality of values generates unresolved (perhaps unresolvable) differences about the role and mission of higher education. When purposes are subject to debate, agreement on the processes used and the results achieved is unlikely.

Values (Virtues and Vices) in Decision Making

Paul L. Dressel

This chapter is intended to be both philosophical and practical. It is philosophical in the sense that it represents a personal philosophy, a development of a point of view about action research, evaluation, or institutional research developed over a period of years in which (or so it seems to me) there has been an increasing emphasis on the need for evaluation but also an increasing inability to so direct the planning, execution, interpretation, and application of evaluation to bring decisions about social action programs, including education, into the rational sphere. The philosophical aspects of these concerns, accordingly, are a venture into consideration of the preconceptions or assumptions and the human yearnings, biases, and deficiencies that often make the task of the evaluator precarious and unrewarding. The evaluator is often rendered impotent by suspicions of his motives, by criticisms of the accuracy or adequacy of his data or by denial of the appropriateness of the techniques used. The most difficult of all circumstances for the evaluator is found when he is faced with individuals who are confident that the truth is known and that its implications transcend any empirical investigation.

My remarks here are also meant to be highly practical to the evaluator who inevitably enters into his role with the conviction that his studies and reports will directly determine the decisions that are reached. Too often he expects that administrators, students, faculty, board members, donors, and

R. Wilson (Ed.). *New Directions for Higher Education: Designing Academic Program Reviews,* no. 37.
San Francisco: Jossey-Bass, March 1982.

the general public will welcome the evaluation report and its recommendations, applaud the industry and wisdom of the evaluator, and either rush to carry out his recommendations or promote him to an administrative role to do so. It is essential that the evaluator who would influence decision making through research realize that the research in which he engages, the data collected, and the analysis and interpretation are, in themselves, either forthrightly or subtly influenced by the values of the institution or agency which the evaluator serves. For example, many hours of time may be expended in an analysis of travel expenditures in academic units because some sequence of events has caused public criticism of travel expenses. At the same time, a provost or president who either believes firmly in faculty autonomy or fears faculty reactions may rule out studies of a profusion of courses and unnecessary repetition of these courses from term to term with resulting small sections, high cost, and unreasonably heavy and unnecessary demands on classroom and laboratory space. We regularly waste funds and time on matters of little impact affecting a few persons and carefully avoid those affecting many persons and involving extensive resources.

The university persists, to a large extent, in developing education, on the basis of deferred gratification—that is, on the assumption that several years of seclusion from real life are essential to development of the insights and abilities to deal with reality. But as the range of tasks for which education is expected to prepare individuals has increased, reflecting the increase in heterogeneity and in value orientation of our society, the plurality of values and resulting conflicts in goals and aspirations have generated unresolved (perhaps unresolvable) differences about the role and mission of higher education. When purposes are subject to debate, agreement on the processes used and the results achieved is unlikely.

The Present Scene

The preceding remarks reflect a long-term development in which the essential nature of higher education, as reflected in its purposes, processes, and expected results, has become increasingly unclear and controversial. The end in this development is not yet apparent. Concurrently, it appears that public higher education, once regarded as providing opportunity for the optimal development for each individual as a basis for optimizing that individual's contribution to society has changed in the minds of many persons to an expectation and even a demand that higher education be assured for every individual and that, the opportunity having been assured, its benefits also be assured in the form of status, salary, and power. Yet having moved toward the provision of this assurance by exhorbitant support to institutions, individuals, and likewise by wasteful and ineffective social programs, we find that the costs in terms of ever increasing taxation and an ever increasing national debt are troublesome. The result is that many people now argue that individuals seeking higher education should mortgage their own futures because of the economic benefits that may be expected. We confront one of the irresolvable issues. Is higher education made available primarily for individual advancement, or is it viewed as an obligation of the present society to contribute to the welfare of our youth and to the preservation and improvement of a society of which we are the progenitors?

In the present scene, we are also heavily influenced by the awareness that our natural resources are not inexhaustible. The human race has, through its use of technology, moved from a precarious existence in an environment hardly subject to modification to one in which man has achieved marked success in modifying and utilizing his environment and the resources embedded in it without seriously questioning the ultimate implications of this use or the worth of the results achieved. Humans seeking values through social institutions utilizing resources is a crisp characterization of history. In the era since the New Deal we have had a series of deals in which, supported both by dubious economic theories and false interpretations of them, we have embarked upon a program of expenditures and resource utilization that turns out not only to be wasteful, but also conducive to duplicity and dishonesty simply because the magnitude of the operations and the expenditures involved transcends our ability to manage or monitor them. The demand for accountability is overdue and necessary. Unfortunately, it comes too frequently from those who have not themselves demonstrated accountability and who would impose accountability in terms of a value system inappropriate to and perhaps even incompatible with the enterprise to be evaluated.

Insistence upon increased productivity, program budgets, and cost benefit analyses in universities is symptomatic. Even more unfortunately, these demands fall more heavily upon the universities than upon those agencies of state and federal government that have been ineffective and wasteful. Inevitably, many administrators and faculty members resent the negative implications and resist the demands and controls. Under these circumstances, any attempt at rigorous evaluation (internal or external) arouses tensions. Indeed, any attempt to develop an educational program or to evaluate it and modify or eliminate it not only threatens jobs and egos, but also runs into value conflicts that tend, in the present day, to be attended by such suspicion, conflict, and appeals that either no action is taken or that the compromise achieved by mollifying the concerns of the loudest and most recalcitrant protestants only increases the procedural complications and costs without resolving the original issues. Students, faculty, alumni, governing board members, administrative officers, executive, legislative, and judicial phases of government, and a host of special interest groups request or demand change or the abrogation or modification of proposed change. One hears disparate demands, such as that an individual living in a community in which there is a university ought to have the right to study anything desired at that university. Another equally unreasonable demand is that every educational institution ought to have the right to offer its programs in whatever modes seem appropriate to the faculty at the institution. Still another is that the university should have the right to expand into new programs and activities as justified by demands or as seen as essential by the faculty and the administration for the development and enhancement of the institution itself. In contrast to these views, as the move to state coordination and control amply indicates, there are those who view educational institutions (even the private ones) as serving society and having an obligation to do this within a set of goals and controls which ensure that the total higher education enterprise contributes to society within a framework of broad social commitment, including responsible use of resources.

If our value problems were solely conflicts in the values themselves, there might be some expectation that the development of sensitivity to value differences and respect for them could, in a democratic society, lead to a series of compromises that would establish priorities and equities so that a majority at least could see that rationality can and must adapt to value differences. We might also recognize that value differences are themselves to be expected and indeed essential to an open society in which individuals can develop their unique capacities and achieve thereby both personal development and significant contribution to the social order. However, even when there is extensive agreement on a value there is usually disagreement on its precise meaning in terms of actions and procedures to achieve it and on the nature of the desired results. In the present scene perhaps no single value has caused more discussion, legislation, court intervention, and destructive action than the widely accepted value of equality and its associated concerns with equity and fairness. If, on one hand, the policies and procedures used in accepting students or hiring faculty must be fair, and if, on the other hand, the results of the operation of these policies must demonstrate representativeness in the presence of members of minority groups, has everyone been treated fairly? How and by whom is such a judgment rendered? And how does one deal fairly with the bureaucrat who, inflated with his own self-importance and omniscience, would impose equality at the cost of quality?

Higher education was, and still is, seen by some people as providing individuals with an understanding of the past in the firm conviction that understanding of the past and of the achievements of man in the past will almost certainly develop an individual capable of dealing effectively with the present and the future. There are still others who view education as a full-time living experience that must be oriented to the present and that fostering the fullest development of each individual, including the willingness and ability to work with other individuals, will enable those so educated to develop their own future free of the limitations of the past. And there are yet others who have viewed education always as a preparation for the future and therefore would mold the education of the present in the light of both predictions and aspirations for the future. At the same time, the elaboration of our institutions of education and the range of activities carried on have resulted in so many positions and benefits for those directly involved that education, once seen solely as a means to other ends, has become, for many, and end in itself to be controlled and directed to the immediate benefit of those involved. In so doing, it seems to me that this new approach has only recognized and improved upon the conviction of many faculty members that the university should be run for the benefit of the faculty.

Truisms or Assumptions

What has thus far been said is prelude. I move now to the statement of a series of truisms or assumptions within the framework of which I believe individuals and society operate. Institutions of higher education, despite their commitment to higher values, also operate within this framework. Since each of the statements is relatively brief and largely self-explanatory, I offer them without comment other than some subsequent indications of their relevance in evaluation.

1. Every human decision, consciously or unconsciously, is based upon personal or social values.
2. Values are those beliefs or commitments of importance or worth to individuals that influence their thoughts, actions, and goals in various ways at various times.
3. Values may be highly abstract (truth, for example) or highly concrete (a new and more attractive entrance to the president's house).
4. The prized diversity in American higher education and the pluralistic nature of our society assure continuing disagreements both in the values themselves and in specific implications of even those values that are commonly accepted.
5. The diversity of values in our society reflects both the self-interests of individuals and groups and the natural but self-delusive tendency to evoke an authoritative basis for preferred values that support individual or group aspirations.
6. Issues involving disparate value commitments are never finally solved. They are only temporarily resolved until such time as changing values, changing personnel, or shifting power balances generate a reconsideration. Hence compromises are necessary but seldom entirely satisfactory either as operative policies or as resolutions of issues.
7. Values ultimately are relative (rather than absolute) both in abstract formulation, in application, and in priority. They are matters of tradition, of personal preference, of social acceptability, of authority, or a combination thereof.
8. Values can be divided into virtues and vices, but since a vice may be only a virtue carried to an extreme, there may be no clear and

accepted distinction. Yet the attempt to impose distinctions poses one of our major problems with values. In one extreme, anything pleasurable may be labeled a vice and self-mortification may be viewed as a virtue.

9. Self-deception is both a virtue and a vice in that it permits one to support on high principle that policy or action deemed most beneficial to others.

The preceding assumptions reflect what some may regard as a cynical but what I personally regard as a realistic view of mankind's involvement with and commitment to values. In particular, it seems to me that faculty members and administrators in higher education engage in a great deal of self-deception in that they come to operate upon the principle that what is good for themselves and the institution is also good for students and society. At times this view involves some deception of students and society as to just what the institution is doing and why. A part of the self-deception is that the belief that either students or society can long be deceived. The operation of these assumptions can be most readily seen by discussion of some of the main value conflicts in higher education.

Major Value Conflicts in Higher Education

I would place foremost among the continuing major value conflicts that involving liberal education versus professional or vocational education. In reality, I think there need not be, indeed is not, a conflict between liberal and vocational education. Yet it is a measure of our values that we insist upon making a distinction between an education that is value oriented (liberal education) and an education that is action oriented (vocational or professional education). It is as though we assume that what one does for a living must either ignore or deny the values that we believe to be the most fundamental. In the name of a broad liberal education we impose upon students a set of required courses, and we assert that it is good to impose these requirements because otherwise students would avoid significant areas of knowledge or would take the easy way out. By denying choice, we seek to develop the ability to make wise choices.

The liberal versus vocational education conflict is also apparent in the conflict over the weighting of humanities and science requirements. The sciences involve acquiring knowledge relative to aspects of the world and are generally oriented to using, as well as acquiring, knowledge. Some humanists find that this places science well outside the domain of liberal education and hence view a liberal education as concentrating in the classics and the humanities. And some scientists are perfectly satisfied that this be true, for it permits the scientist to view education as specialization. The issues here have been argued for centuries and will continue to be argued with no resolution in view. The difficulty is that few faculty members are truly liberally educated.

A second major value conflict in higher education revolves around the issue of campus residency versus social involvement. Many colleges and universities still hold to the ideal that the attainment of a baccalaureate degree requires a four-year immersion in a campus-based program despite the fact that travel, entertainment facilities, the relationship of education to national and social needs, and the vast expansion of knowledge have long since rendered a four-year monastic seclusion both an anachronism and an impossibility. Some colleges still holding to this concept have themselves irretrievably damaged the concept itself by introduction of work-study programs, study abroad, and community service activities. Each of these activities requires varying amounts of absence from the campus and remains largely uncorrelated with campus living and study. Some individuals have carried this further in that they have come to believe that the most significant education involves a combination of reading and reflection along with active involvement in life and work. Thus we have the phenomena of institutions giving credit for life experiences. Traditional degree designations, including the Ph.D., are granted for an array of activities, the most notable feature of which is absence from the campus. Frequently, though not necessarily, this means both a failure to develop either the ability to acquire knowledge or competency in using it. Hutchins, in his facetious and irritating way, once suggested that those individuals seeking a degree from a college be awarded the degree immediately, sent home, and those remaining would then engage in serious study. We are far closer to this than he anticipated.

A third major value conflict in higher education resides in the curriculum itself. In earlier discussions of the conflict between liberal and vocational education, the issues involved in a limited and required curriculum, on the one hand, and an extensive and elective curriculum, on the other, were noted. I am reminded of a venture in which I was involved with Earl McGrath some years ago. We identified a number of colleges and departments within them that demonstrated great variation in the number of courses and credits. In fact, some departments in a given discipline offered undergraduate courses and credits totalling four and five times those offered in other departments. When the chairmen of these departments were queried as to the rationale for the offerings, we found it curious and amusing that the common rationale was that because most of their students went on to graduate school they must be well prepared in the fundamentals. Both chairmen were supporting complete coverage of everything of importance. This vain conception of completeness has brought about an extension and specialization of the curriculum to the point where every phase of a discipline must be represented. This irrational expansion of program offerings has led to superficiality and incoherence. Course proliferation is a coarse approach to defining an education.

Another major value conflict in higher education has to do with the institutional role, mission, and level of program offered. We have already referred to this in one way or another with regard to curriculum, degree programs, and discipline. I recently conducted a study viewing the differences in patterns of state coordination found in Ohio, Indiana, and Wisconsin, with some reflection on the relationship of these three to other forms of state coordination and control (Dressel, 1980). I concluded that some form of coordination is essential to hamper the unbridled autonomy of institutions, which leads each to seek gradually to become everything for everybody while continuously asserting that no quality institution can or should do everything that somebody expects. In reality, program decisions are often reduced to whether or not funding is available. I have talked with a few presidents who were able to see the relationship of their several institutions in a state as a cooperative and reinforcing one in which decisions must be made relative to needs and resources rather than to local, institutional, and faculty expectations or demands. Yet some of these individuals were quite forthright in saying that denial of a progrm of some importance to faculty, institutional board members, alumni, or local citizens could be suicidal for an administrator. The experience of public denunciation of state coordinating or control board action conjoined with a private expression of satisfaction for that same action conveys something of the deception engendered by these role and mission conflicts. The insistence upon autonomy, on one hand, and the irresponsibility in use of autonomy, on the other, make it evident that the institution of higher education, which should represent the greatest human effort and success in combining rationality with value commitments and social responsibility, represents an unrealizable dream.

Values and the Evaluator

Previous remarks have repeatedly emphasized the role of values in planning, executing, and interpreting evaluations. Even when there is conscious recognition of specific value commitments, this recognition seems only to introduce a subjective element into evaluation, which decreases the acceptability of the results to others. Objectivity in evaluation is a value in achieving valid results and in gaining acceptance of them. I identify three types of values that are involved in any evaluation. The first is an intrinsic value that may be viewed as quality, goodness, excellence, or merit untrammeled by time, place, or circumstances. Truth is such a value. The second type is an extrinsic or *context value*. This refers to the worth of a concept or object in a particular situation. The honest man hardly regards a "white lie" as an intrinsic value but may find it entirely acceptable in some circumstances. The wise husband does not express profound dislike of his wife's new dress. A given value may be either intrinsic or context depending upon circumstances. The adage that cleanliness is next to godliness views cleanliness as an intrinsic value. Cleanliness promoted to asepsis is essential in the hosptial operating room. The third type of value is a *process value*, a commitment to maintenance of existing processes, rules, requirements, and modes of instruction that actually have little relevance to either intrinsic or context values.

Objectivity, to whatever extent it is possible, is a desirable attribute of an evaluation report destined to assist others in understanding a problem and reaching a decision about it. Objectivity helps to achieve acceptability, but the maintenance of the objectivity is difficult if any attempt is made to interpret evidence and explore its implications. Even the attribution of intrinsic, context, or process values to a concept may arouse some disagreement. One who fully accepts a truth is seldom completely objective about it. The evaluator cannot resolve these value conflicts, yet he or she must assist in identifying the value differences and suggest some grounds for resolving them. Over time, on most campuses, inequities arise in the allocation of resources to various units, in great part, because opportunism, expediency, and competition with other institutions obscure the intrinsic values involved. Fundamental decisions are not made but rather result from small but cumulative commitments over time. A new and unnecessary program is recognized and approved only after the courses and faculty required are in place. The evaluation can do little about these cumulative commitments because they proceed without planning and rational decisions.

The evaluator must be mindful that sound policies and decisions are always made in reference to the imposition of some set of values on the data. Many studies grow out of a concern about the *representativeness* of the institutional population on such factors as race, sex, geographical sources of students, and the institutional sources of degrees held by faculty. *Equitability* (or *fairness*), a second value, extends the concept of representativeness to asking the grounds upon which representativeness is determined, but equitability goes further to consider the reward system, including salaries, promotions, and assignments. A third value is that of *feasibility* or *practicability*. Some unknown wise man observed that you can go where you will only if you choose to go where you can. Thus studies proposing changes that require excessive time or resources are generally of limited value and possibly, by denial, become destructive of morale. Feasibility also involves the idea of planning a gradual movement to a desired goal when disruption and lack of funds would make that goal unfeasible and probably undesirable as an immediate accomplishment.

A fourth value is that of *suitability*. This value is closely related to the concepts of mission, role, and scope that are often discussed in state planning today. Suitability involves consistency, interaction, mutual support, and building strength in contrast to recommendations that extend and possibly weaken an institution by internal competition and strife.

A fifth value is that of *necessity*. Necessity is often invoked in the present day when equity or feasibility should be the real concern. Necessity frequently involves the correction of deficiencies, but the correction of deficiencies is a matter of priority, opportunity, and resource availability. The necessity of simultaneously launching a wide range of social programs and of maintaining worldwide involvement is the origin of much of the difficulty that the United States faces today.

A sixth value is that of *efficiency*. Efficiency has often been ridiculed in higher education discussions and sometimes placed in opposition to effectiveness. Nothing can be efficient unless it is effective, but overemphasis on efficiency can destroy or weaken effectiveness. One does not maximize efficiency; rather, it is optimized to achieve an acceptable level of effectiveness.

Once it becomes clear that values provide the basis for evaluation, it is evident that evaluation is far more than data collection. Evaluation reports and recommendations cannot be based solely on the values of those conducting the study or of those who request it. How does one decide whether an operation is efficient? How does one discern the quality of an institution? What are the criteria for judging the feasibility of a project?

There are at least five distinctive bases (or process values) for judgment. The first of these is *comparison* with relevant data from similar institutions. What is relevant and what institutions are similar? Tuition and fee charges are adjusted with an eye to the charges in other institutions. Some comparisons are solely informative in reference to established norms. For library holdings, standards suggested by various authorities have become the basis for normative judgments of adequacy or inadequacy.

Theoretical models (the second basis for judgment) can sometimes be derived from explicit assumptions. For example, at various times individuals have argued that the percentage of tenured faculty should not be higher than 67 percent, and that the range across units should be from 50 to 67 percent. There have also been attempts at relating course offerings in departments to the number of majors or the total curriculum of the college to its enrollment by stating certain assumptions about student-faculty ratio, class size, and other factors. Obtaining agreement on assumptions is difficult. Furthermore, if the model requires a major change in practices, it will certainly be rejected by some units as inapplicable.

A third basis for judgment is the *application of absolute standards*. For example, student records should be complete and accurate. Even occasional errors would influence judgments about the effectiveness of the registrar.

A fourth basis for decisions is *cost benefit* or *cost effectiveness analysis*. For many years, evaluation and institutional research proceeded with little attention to dollar costs, apparently assuming that if dollars could not immediately be found, the next student increment would bring the needed resources. The prevalent view was that instrinsic value commitments should be not soiled by concern about costs. Today cost benefit analysis appears to be a highly pragmatic basis for decisions, but it is difficult to apply because of the resistance aroused when costs are introduced into academic discussions. Furthermore, the faculty has program convictions and is unwilling to consider the comparative benefits and costs of alternatives. The usual result is that fund availability determines programs and effectiveness is never known. The recurrent complaint of university presidents that lack of funds threatens quality raises an interesting paradox: When quality is unknown, the effect of lowering financial support is also unknown.

A fifth decision-making value, another highly pragmatic one, is *consensus*. In a democratic society, there is a tendency to feel that a high level of agreement on a course of action indicates that it is appropriate. Whether it is the *best* one or the right one remains unknown. The majority can be wrong. This possibility places upon the majority an obligation to maintain fairness and equitability for the minority. Whose conception of equity and fairness should be operative? History effectively demonstrates that minorities have often dominated majorities. The fundamental basis for consensus as a value is its feasibility. A decision can be made operative if a large number of people endorse it. Achieving consensus (often a bare majority) involves a series of compromises so that the ultimate solution is not entirely satisfactory to anyone, and many persons, confident in their own personal commitments and values, do not feel bound by consensus.

By disseminating pertinent data, evaluators can contribute to making the achievement of a consensus a more rational process than it would be otherwise. The timing of a study is important. If the study is not launched until someone has demanded it, the scope and nature of the study will be compromised simply because of time pressures. However, at a point where some decision must be made, evaluations are likely to have more impact than when a decision can be avoided.

The task of the evaluator is that of identifying intrinsic values that motivate faculty members, students, administrators, and others. The evaluator must also consider the context and develop a list of possible alternatives arising out of contextual factors. The evaluation itself must reflect an awareness of and clearly identify process values. Finally, the evaluator needs to be aware of his or her values and of the role of these values in determining the nature of the evaluation and the process used.

The prime role of the evaluator is not that of making a decision or even of promoting a particular one. Evaluation should help educators become sensitive to their values and responsibilities and to those of others. The purpose of evaluation is to encourage value-based decision making so that the university can be seen as emulating the examined life rather than drifting or making decisions only under pressure or continually taking such actions to advance its own prestige. Effective evaluation should encourage reflection and long-term planning at least as much as it facilitates concurrent decision making.

Advice to Evaluators

The preceding remarks about the involvement of values in decision making contain numerous implications regarding the stance and role of evaluators. However, since this chapter is primarily directed to evaluators, it is desirable to make the implicit explicit. I shall do so, but with the warning that my conceptions and injunctions arise out of a personal value system that undergirds this entire statement.

1. The evaluator who identifies a problem or an ill-functioning process and would independently initiate a study of it should identify and examine those personal preconceptions and values which led to that conclusion. He or she should then undertake to determine the views (preconceptions and values) of others directly involved who will be affected by evaluation and possible change. If they see no problem or exhibit general satisfaction with the status quo, a study designed to bring about immediate change is likely to be wasted effort, whereas efforts directed to arousing concern through bringing to light inequities resulting from present practices may be effective over time. Sponsorship by an advisory committee will assist this development in that it relieves the evaluator of the sole responsibility of questioning the judgments of others.

2. The evaluator, in undertaking studies requested by administrators, faculty committees, or others, should seek to clarify the precise nature of the generating concern. Requests for studies may be the equivalent of tabling an issue when the assumptions and values underlying various resolutions of it are unclear and controversial. When groups are unwilling to identify or are incapable of resolving value conflicts, objective evaluation reports are more likely to be rejected on the grounds of inadequate, inaccurate, or inappropriate data, misuse of analytical procedures, or unjustified or improper interpretations than they are to achieve acceptance and generate a consensus. Thus the evaluator faces a choice between using evaluation as a process to facilitate a decision and as a process of involvement designed to clarify issues and foster a consensus reflected in, rather than generated by, the evaluation.

3. The evaluator should avoid taking on the role of decision maker. An evaluative report ought to consider alternative interpretations of data and various possible resolutions of the problems identified. The evaluator ought also to explore the consequences (both expected and unanticipated) of various actions. This phase of the report should include perceptions and concerns of others rather than those of the evaluator or individuals closely associated with the evaluation function. To the extent that the report recognizes concerns and objectives and deals systematically with them, it will facilitate deliberation and decision making rather than become an object of contention. Particularly, the evaluator should attempt to project impacts upon students, alumni, and influential external individuals and organizations related to the university. Faculty members tend to be preoccupied with personal and institutional unit impacts.

4. The experienced evaluator with recognized expertise in a problem area may express personal views upon request or by individual initiative, but should separate these views from the formal report. The logic and values supporting the evaluator's views should be made clear to demonstrate an approach to the formulation of views and decision making worthy of emulation by those formally assigned the responsibilities for decision making. The ideal in evaluation is for each decision maker to become something of an eval-

uator. The professional evaluator recognizes that encroachment by the evaluator into the decision making role is likely to destroy both the quality of the evaluation and the reputation of the evaluator for objectivity and for constructive assistance in providing useful information and analyses.

5. The evaluator should give special attention to the cost implications of any process or program alteration. Costs involve not only dollars but also impacts on other aspects of local institutional operation and on other institutions in the system of which the institution is a part. Programs or improvements forgone are costs to an instituion just as much as are actual dollars spent. Priorities are involved in any decision. These priorities involve not only choices among changes or innovations in programs, policies, but also the containment, curtailment, or elimination of others. Decisions on one matter can seldom be completely isolated from others, but committees and administrators, by the limited nature of their charges and authority, are prone to ignore side reactions and broader implications.

6. Evaluators should continually emphasize that operational, policy, and program changes in a college or university will be ineffective unless those affected by them understand and accept the rationale involved and value the anticipated benefits. Changes that are highly critical and punitive in tone and nature are not likely to achieve acceptance or the results desired. Few changes, especially those that appear to be far reaching in nature, achieve the results projected by their enthusiastic proponents. Evaluators, by placing their evaluation reports in a broad context and by remarking on similar developments in other institutions, can encourage a realistic and developmental approach to decision making.

In summary, I believe that the role of evaluators is that of encouraging a rational value-based approach to decision making. This is a sensitive and difficult task, and it poses an equally sensitive and difficult task in evaluating the evaluators, for it emphasizes the positive impact of an evaluation report upon decision makers as much or more than it does the technical excellence of the evaluation.

References

Dressel, P. L. (Ed.). *New Directions for Institutional Research: The Autonomy of Public Colleges,* no. 26. San Francisco: Jossey-Bass, 1980.

Paul L. Dressel is currently professor of university research at Michigan State University. He gave up all administrative duties a few years ago to devote more time to research and writing after having served as an administrator for some thirty-six years. His contributions to the field of higher education are well known nationally and include several books in the areas of evaluation, curriculum development, and institutional research.

A successful review of program quality requires a clear understanding by all participants of what is meant by "quality" and careful attention in advance to assessment techniques.

Assessing Program Quality

Melvin D. George

One of the many possible reasons for undertaking a program review process is to help determine the quality of programs. Such determination of quality may be for the purpose of self-improvement, with the results to be used by the unit being reviewed. On the other hand, some assessment of the program against an external standard, with corrective action imposed by an outside agent, might be the motivation. In any event, program reviews conducted primarily to assess and improve program quality may differ significantly from program reviews conducted to make decisions about retrenchment, to assess leadership of the department, or to develop a long-range institutional plan. For example, a program review conducted by a department for self-directed improvement of its program offerings would undoubtedly be quite different from one conducted by the president of the institution to determine areas for budget reduction. Obviously, the level of enthusiasm of the unit, the kinds of data that may be provided, and the impact of review results will be quite different in these two situations. Quality assessment should not be ignored in a retrenchment process, but the two distinct motivations of improvement and reduction in resources will generally involve somewhat different processes and may produce quite different results.

In general, no program review can proceed effectively unless there is some clear understanding of the purpose of the review. That understanding must, to the largest extent possible, be shared by all participants in the process. Thus, much of what is said here about program review for the primary

R. Wilson (Ed.). *New Directions for Higher Education: Designing Academic Program Reviews,* no. 37. San Francisco: Jossey-Bass, March 1982.

purpose of assessing and improving program quality may not apply to program reviews conducted for other purposes. Similarly, in reviews undertaken for different reasons, the component of quality assessment may be present in a form that differs from that chosen for a review that has such assessment as its sole or driving purpose.

Assume then that one wishes to undertake a program review to determine the quality of the program. Throughout this chapter, "program" will generally mean a budgetary unit, such as a department, rather than a degree or curricular program. This will not always be the appropriate way to review activities, but since a budgetary unit is one that controls hiring, space, equipment, and other important aspects of institutional activities, such units may be the appropriate way to organize reviews. This discussion is also confined to academic program review, although it is increasingly important to institute and develop processes for the review of the quality of support service units as well.

What is meant by the word "quality"? It may be novel to stop to examine the meaning of that word, but much of the confusion about assessing program quality results from an inability or unwillingness to try to determine exactly what is to be assessed. It does not seem possible that one oculd develop an appropriate assessment technique for something that is not defined. Academic quality, a concept difficult to define, has been used to mean many things, some of which are explicit and others of which are unspoken and unexamined.

Several Approaches to Quality

Undoubtedly the most common view of academic quality is one that might be called "mystical" (Astin, 1980). In this approach, academics are the priesthood, the keepers of the secrets of the god Quality, none of which can be revealed to the laity. This view is usually apparent when faculty and administrators invoke the word "quality" in budget requests and speeches; fortunately, hardly anyone notices that the speaker does not bother to say what it is or how someone can tell when it is present. If pressed, the speaker might reply that the concept is so complicated that no one outside academia can understand it or recognize it. If that is the best that can be done, academics ought to stop talking about quality to avoid insulting the intelligence of their listeners.

Another common way of thinking about quality is to equate it with reputation. The assessments of quality done by Alan Cartter in 1966, followed by those of Roose and Andersen (1970), were examples of the determination of quality by amalgamation of the opinions of peers. There are a number of issues and questions raised by this approach, of course. An obvious one is how the peer group is selected. Another common criticism of this view of quality is that the level of knowledge of the peers about the program and their own definitions of quality are usually completely unknown. Despite these valid criticisms, however, it certainly is true that reputational rankings that have the concurrence of large numbers of peers must have some merit, and they undoubtedly make some contribution to a general understanding of the degree of success of the program in question. Obviously, the more the participating peers are informed about the program, the greater will be the significance of the results.

Lawrence and Green (1980) summarize a number of results of studies that correlate various quantifiable factors with such reputational rankings. They point out, for example, that the size of department accounts for a significant fraction of the variation in Cartter's ranking. So, such rankings may be informative, but must certainly be approached with caution and employed with care.

Regional accrediting bodies have generally seemed to stress that quality refers to the degree of conformance between goals and actions. This understanding of quality reflects a correct assumption that there are various kinds of institutions and different kinds of programs, and not all of them ought to behave in exactly the same way, given their varied purposes. The North Central Association's *Handbook on Accreditation,* for example, states that: "Voluntary institutional accreditation . . . arose in response to the need for the establishment of some agency to attest to the quality of educational institutions"(p. 7). It states further: "Accreditation is a status granted by a regional accrediting commission which indicates that an institution is offering its students on a satisfactory level the educational opportunities implied in its objectives" (p. 29). These two statements tie together quality and the satisfactory achievement of objectives. Even more explicit is a statement of Kenneth Young (1976, p. 133), president of the Council on Postsecondary Accreditation (COPA), to the annual meeting of the Council of Graduate Schools: "If accreditation can be defined in twenty-five words or less, that definition would be: Accreditation is a process that attempts to evaluate and encourage institutional quality." Of course, an institution should match its actions with its stated purposes. However, this approach does not explicitly include any examination of the appropriateness of any of the goals. An institution that has as its goal the granting of degrees in the easiest manner possible and that has carried out that goal by awarding everyone a diploma upon registration might be said to have achieved an acceptable level of quality. However, neither the North Central Association nor most people in higher education would be comfortable with that extreme position.

Many people have equated level of program quality with the magnitude of various program input variables or resources. For instance, quite commonly academics tacitly identify quality level with the amount of funds available. This is an unspoken, but probably not undetected, theme of many budget presentations made by public university presidents to legislators and governors. The assumption is made that whatever quality is, it is linearly related to money, and hence an increase in financing must *a fortiori* produce a higher quality program. However, as George H. Callcott (1980), former vice-chancellor for academic affairs at the University of Maryland at College Park, has observed, several schools have high faculty salaries without being generally perceived as having high-quality programs. So the relationship is not as linear, apparently, as college presidents might like legislators to believe. Indeed, Minter and Bowen (1980) report that when presidents were asked to assess trends in various indicators of the health of their institutions in 1979–80, most said that they were losing ground financially, but that academic conditions in their institutions were improving as was the quality of student services. Those responses might suggest that cutting funds available to a program will improve its quality.

Other input variables that have been identified with program quality include qualifications of students admitted and enrolling, percentage of faculty members holding terminal degrees, condition of physical plant, and so forth. Measurement of such resources has probably constituted the most significant portion of program assessment procedures oriented toward quality. Most people in higher education believe that some input variables, such as large libraries and modern equipment, are highly correlated with whatever is meant by quality, and since these things are usually reasonably easy to measure, they become handy tools in program review. Indeed they are a useful and essential part of the assessment of program quality, but many would argue that they do not constitute the full answer to the problem.

One relatively uncommon way of thinking about quality is to identify it with certain process characteristics. For example, one may assert that quality refers to the intellectual climate of an institution, the methodology of teaching (large lectures, small classes, television, computer-assisted instruction), or the nature of faculty-student relationships. Callcott has stressed two such process characteristics—faculty morale and the institutional will to excellence—as being perhaps the most significant factors that determine the excellence of an institution. By morale, he means an institution's self-image, its belief in itself, the belief that what is being done is worthwhile and valuable. In the process area, there is a lot of folklore, well illustrated by a newly elected governor who said in his victory statement on election night: "We promised to improve the quality of education by reducing class sizes, and we will do so." Now it is obvious that he has been listening to academics who have maintained that quality and class size are inextricably and directly linked. Whether or not that is the case is subject to debate. At the same time, no one would deny that a demoralized faculty can surely not be teaching or producing knowledge effectively. And so, as with inputs, process indicators can help to define quality.

Finally, and increasingly commonly in recent years, quality has been identified with certain outputs or products. One has only to listen to the calls for required examinations for high school graduation to realize the extent to which many lay persons and some educators have become more convinced that quality must mean measurable value added, whether in knowledge, ethical standards, or vocational skills. In the extreme, this conception embraces the view that it does not matter what the imputs are or what the process might be; only the results count. Carrying this approach to its extreme might result in a classroom in which students are beaten to force them to learn multiplication tables. But surely the proponents of a definition of quality as the degree of measurable output of knowledge are speaking a part of the truth. Institutional resources, processes, goals, and reputations are surely only worthwhile if, in the long run, the institution helps students learn or produces new knowledge or brings about some other worthwhile outcome. Of course, one of the great overlooked problems with reliance on output measures is that it remains unclear how to modify a program to raise those measures.

And so there are varying approaches to, or definitions of, quality. These sample descriptions indicate that operational differences in assessment methodology are required, depending on which of these approaches is adopted. If the president of a college believes that quality means reputation among peers and a department assesses its quality by the size of its budgets and classes, both parties think they are talking about quality, but they will pass each other like ships at sea in the night, without a glimmer of communication.

Nearly all of these notions of quality have some validity and contribute to a clear understanding of quality. The most important point is that those persons involved must be reasonably clear about what is meant before assessment techniques and procedures are developed. To do otherwise is almost to guarantee confusion, frustration, and contention.

An Operational Definition of Quality

Quality is certainly related, as the dictionary definition makes clear, to the notion of a standard; someone has to set that standard. It also is clear that quality is a relative term. One does not talk about a program that has quality, constrasted with another that does not; normally one speaks of higher or lower quality, implying a predetermined scale of relative worth. Thus, an appropriate assessment of quality consists of two parts—setting or acknowledging a standard, and determining how various aspects of a program measure up against that standard.

In an educational setting, an adequate understanding of quality at an institution must begin with the acceptance and articulation of one or more goals traditionally associated with higher education. These goals might include fostering intellectual excitement, preparing students for vocations, or adding to society's knowledge. The purposes of an institution or program must be more than arbitrary ones determined at the whim of an institution; they must be acceptable. One can legitimately ask how to determine which goals or purposes are valid and which are not, but it is surely a waste of time to pretend that there is not a range of commonly accepted goals or purposes from which an institution should choose. The initial selection of goals must be done honestly and realistically, lest the purposes chosen be stock ones that bear little relation to the intent of those involved in the program. In addition, institutional or program goals should be subjected to external review for verification that they indeed are acceptable. Such an external review does not require specific knowledge of the institution (or of the program); it is not as uncertain a process or one as open to question as is reputational rankings of programs.

To raise the quality of a program then is to increase either the range of acceptable purposes that it attempts to achieve or to raise the degree of success with which it meets existing purposes. To put it another way, to improve quality means either to expand the values reflected in the program or to modify the program so that it more fully attains the standards embodied in an unchanged set of goals, or both. To measure that attainment, one must use a variety of techniques, including possibly peer review and the assessment of a combination of input, process, and output variables, using both quantitative data and nonquantifiable, descriptive measures and materials. To assess program quality, therefore, is to determine the acceptable purposes reflected in the program and the degree to which each of those is achieved.

The first step in such an assessment is to establish a set of goals or purposes for the program. Next the resources, process, and output variables that are germane to those particular purposes must be identified. For example, scholarly publication productivity may not be relevant in a community college. This identification should be carried out without reference to the subsequent question of how the variables will be measured. However, in selecting variables, one should keep in mind the possible actions to be taken to improve quality after the review. Implications for potential changes ought to influence the choice.

As an example of the process of selecting relevant variables, the Graduate Record Examination Board and the Council of Graduate Schools in the United States have done a great deal of work on how to assess quality in graduate programs. Using the opinions of graduate deans across the country, a list of program characteristics judged important to quality has been developed (Clark, 1980). This list includes such items as academic training of the faculty, satisfaction of the students, library resources, admissions policies, and professional accomplishments of graduates, together with faculty morale and student-faculty interaction. This list includes resource variables, process characteristics, and output factors.

Graduate programs are mentioned here because perhaps more work has been done in this program area than in others. But the basic methodology applies to community colleges, to liberal arts schools, and to professional programs. Indeed, in any institution and at any level, similar lists of relevant variables can be developed from the established purposes and values. Lawrence and Green (1980), for example, refer to several studies of quality in undergraduate and professional programs that employ criteria that might be used in such a list. The program evaluator must ensure that the list is carefully and thoughtfully selected.

The final step is to determine how to measure each of the relevant variables in the program. At this stage, careful thought must be given to the question of how much quantitative data will be needed, what kinds of nonquantitative materials (such as peer opinions or narrative descriptions) would be useful, and how all this material will be interpreted and judged. These determinations can be another area of problems and potential confusion.

In some quarters, it is felt that no numerical (quantitative) indicator can, by definition, convey qualitative information (that is, information about quality). Alscamp (1976) notes that administrators fail miserably to specify the connection between things that are numerable and the illusive notion of quality. In fact, some people feel that quality determinations must of necessity involve nonquantitative information only—a position that seems clearly to be unsupportable. Although judgment must always be involved, quantitative data surely play in important role in assessing quality.

On the other hand, some prophets have worshipped quantitative indices as the source of all understanding about quality. For them, all judgment is suspect. However, such views are simplistic and probably dangerous. In the introduction to the first ACE study of quality in graduate education, Alan Cartter (1966, p. 4) wrote:

> No single index—be it size of endowment, number of books in the library, publication record of the faculty, level of faculty salaries, or numbers of Nobel laureates on the faculty, Guggenheim fellows, member of the National Academy of Sciences, National Merit scholars in the undergraduate college, or Woodrow Wilson fellows in the graduate school—nor any combination of measures is sufficient to estimate adequately the true worth of an educational institution.
>
> The factors mentioned above are often referred to as "objective" measures of quality. On reflection, however, it is evident that they are for the most part "subjective" measures once removed. Distinguished fellows, Nobel laureates, and National Academy members are selected by peer groups on the basis of subjective assessments, faculty salaries are determined by someone's subjective appraisal, and endowments are the result of philanthropic judgments. Number of volumes in the library, though more readily quantifiable, is a factor of little value in measuring institutional resources unless one can make a qualitative judgment about the adequacy of the holdings.

Normally, a variety of measurements of relevant program variables is used, some quantitative and some nonquantitative. Because evaluation is not exact in science, a deliberate decision to employ a variety of techniques may produce results that are more reliable and more credible than any single measurement device might produce.

If this general approach is adopted, a difficult last step, which is sometimes overlooked, remains; that is, all of this information will have to be integrated to lead to a set of judgments. Such judgments are both particular (interpreting an individual piece of information developed during the program review) and general (weighing and balancing various and sometimes contradictory data, impressions, and descriptions coming out of the assessment process).

No matter how much numerical data may be part of a program review process, the conclusions always must be derived through the exercise of judgment. Even if there is only one quantity measured in such an excercise, a decision on whether a given number is "good" or "bad" is a nonquantifiable judgment. In various circumstances, these judgments will be exercised by an individual; in others, they will be the collective wisdom of some program review board of regents.

We may as well clarify from the start that judgment will be involved; to pretend that a formula calculation can led to a valid conclusion is to hide the judgment in jargon. These judgments will of necessity be shaped by history and circumstance. In advance of the review, the mechanisms for making these judgments and for reaching conclusions must be understood. In some cases, the process will be a private one undertaken by a president. In other cases, a program review committee may decide in advance about ways of weighting ranges of acceptable purposes and measures of their associated variables. It seems always better to have such discussions before a specific case arises, lest the general get lost in the uncertainties and the vicissitudes of the particular.

Final Cautions

Keep two cautions in mind about the measures used in program review. Those undertaking such a review should be aware of the Heisenberg uncertainty principle in physics, which states roughly that the more precisely one tries to measure the position of an electron the less certainly can its momentum be determined, beccause the very act of measurement perturbs the electron.

Certainly the phenomenon that measurement may disturb the thing being measured is also observable in higher education. If administrators count publications, over time they will modify behavior; if they measure the number of degrees granted per year, that attention conveys a message that will influence the institution. One should not ask a question without considering what impact asking that question might have on the program. The unintended consequences can actually destroy the assessment and produce a very different kind of institution from what exists and from what is desired. Some measurements that might be made in a program review process clearly are less likely than others to influence program behavior. For example, determining the quality of institutions or kinds of jobs that graduates enter, measuring the percent of faculty invited to give colloquia at other institutions, and counting citations of papers are all measures less likely to modify behavior than are such measures as number of students enrolled in the program, number of papers published (without reference to length or quality), and grading practices.

The second caution is to be sure that something happens as a result of the review. Program review can flounder on many shoals; one of the most common reasons for its ultimate failure is the well-founded perception of the faculty that the whole effort has been a waste of time, since nothing has happened as a result. If a unit has undertaken the program review for self-improvement, that responsibility, of course, must be placed with the unit. If the review is being conducted outside the unit, the responsible party must know in advance what the mechanisms are for translating the conclusions of the program review into action that will have an impact on the institution. The use of program review depends, as we made clear earlier, on the purpose of the review process. But whatever the purpose, the institution probably had something more in mind than producing reports that sit on a shelf. In the case of the assessment of quality, the ultimate outcome must surely be some action designed either to improve the quality of the program or to reduce the amount of mischief it makes for the institution's reputation.

The process of program review may have benefits for the unit involved without respect to any direct results that may proceed from the review. However, benefits derived from the process usually involve modifications in the program, which are in fact results; if the process itself is the only detectable benefit of the review, it probably is not worth the effort.

Of course, there is one complicating factor at the stage of results: After the program review is completed and decisions have been made about the quality, it is not always clear what modifications to make in the program to produce desired changes in quality. Particularly because human and monetary resources are always limited, the matter of adopting the best strategy to get the most change in quality possible is extraordinarily difficult and complex.

Finally, consider this heretical thought. Is it possible that there is a simple way to come to a good conclusion about program quality? Given the cost of the program review, can one find an easy way to answer the basic question: Is this program really any good? Obviously, this sourcebook is predicated on the assumption that there is no easy way and that it requires experts to instruct people.

But it just may be possible to tell how good a program is by simply walking into the faculty or student coffee room or lounge and listening to the conversation over the course of a day or two. If the talk is about friends, football games, faculty politics, and the weather, most people would go away convinced that this program needs help or deserves a quiet death. If the conversations, on the other hand, are largely about ideas and learning and conjectures in the particular discipline, perhaps one needs few forms and little data to conclude that this department is one that is alive and probably as good as it can be under the circumstances. Perhaps more creative yet simpler assessments of quality than are generally used would go a long way toward making program reviews more cost effective and better accepted by faculty.

References

Astin, A. W. "When Does a College Deserve to be Called 'High Quality'?" *Current Issues in Higher Education*, 1980, *2* (1), 1-9.

Callcott, G. H. "The Costs of Excellence." *University of Maryland Graduate School Chronicle,* April 1980, *13* (3), 2-9.

Cartter, A. M. *An Assessment of Quality in Graduate Education.* Washington, D.C.: American Council on Education, 1966.

Clark, M. J. *Graduate Program Self-Assessment Service Handbook for Users*. Princeton, N.J.: Educational Testing Service, 1980.

Lawrence, J. K., and Green, K. C. *A Question of Quality: The Higher Education Ratings Game.* AAHE-ERIC/Higher Education Research Report No. 5. Washington, D.C.: American Association of Higher Education, 1980.

Minter, W. J., and Bowen, H. R. *Preserving America's Investment in Human Capital.* Washington, D.C.: American Association of State Colleges and Universities, 1980.

North Central Association of Colleges and Schools. *Handbook on Accreditation.* Boulder, Colo.: North Central Association of Colleges and Schools, 1975.

Olscamp, P. J. "Quality, Quantity, and Accountability." *Educational Record*, 1976, *57* (3), 196-201.

Roose, K. D., and Andersen, C. J. *A Rating of Graduate Programs*. Washington, D.C.: American Council on Education, 1970.

Young, K. "Accreditation and Graduate Education." In *Proceedings of the Sixteenth Annual Meeting of the Council of Graduate Schools in the United States.* Washington, D.C.: Council of Graduate Schools, 1976.

Melvin D. George is vice-president for academic affairs and professor of mathematics at the University of Missouri. Previously he has served as vice-president for academic affairs at the University of Mid-America and dean of the College of Arts and Sciences at the University of Nebraska at Lincoln.

An evaluation system should be dynamic, highly interactive, and localized for each institution.

Evaluation Systems Are More Than Information Systems

Larry A. Braskamp

Information is central to the management and policy making of any institution, including public and private colleges and universities. In the administration of higher education institutions, the program review—also known as departmental evaluation or administrative review—is becoming common practice (Clark, 1977). In a recent survey, college presidents indicated that integrating results from program reviews into program planning and budgeting processes is one of their most pressing needs (Patrick and Caruthers, 1980).

A program evaluation system can be designed and implemented at the state level and local institution level and used by a variety of audiences—campus faculty, administrators, governing boards, and state government. In this chapter, the evaluation systems discussed are aimed primarily at helping local officials—administrators and faculty—in the governance and administration of institutions whether for improvement in curriculum, services, or research or reallocation of resources. The evaluation system may also be used to demonstrate accountability to external publics, but this function is secondary.

A formal evaluation system involves the establishment, maintenance, and operation of an information system, defined here as a system that informs users about operating conditions (for example, costs, inputs, and outputs). This information can be used to control and change an organization. Operationally, a typical information system used by managers is performance ori-

R. Wilson (Ed.). *New Directions for Higher Education: Designing Academic Program Reviews,* no. 37. San Francisco: Jossey-Bass, March 1982.

ented because it provides information based on such performance indicators as costs of products and efficiency (Van de Ven and Ferry, 1980).

An evaluation system cannot exist without a good information system, but it is more than an information system. In this chapter, I will first argue that an evaluation system has five major features, two of them specifically related to an information system. These two features are necessary but not sufficient for designing and maintaining an effective evaluation system for local campus use. The remaining three features are required for an effective evaluation system. After discussing the five features, I will briefly describe evaluation systems at two universities with which I have had personal involvement. Finally I will briefly critique these systems as exemplars of evaluation systems.

Features

1. *An information system should reflect the desired social reality of the institution.* Data and information about an organization have symbolic meaning subject to many interpretations. Administrators and faculty understand an institution by the way they describe it. The available information defines the "character of organization decision making. The language available to managers serves to direct their attention, highlight problem areas requiring action, frame appropriate solutions, and justify the eventual choices of action. The design of an information system plays an important part in defining the official language of an organization" (Boland, 1980, p. 3).

The rhetoric of an institution has important policy implications. Administrators and faculty use data and information to reflect selected key dimensions of the institution as an organization. They describe an institution and make important policy decisions on data such as student count, faculty salaries, student credit hours, ACT or SAT scores of entering freshmen, instructional costs by discipline, and enrollment projections. In short, an information system influences the management structure, the information flow in an organization, the policy-making processes within the organization, and the power of constituencies within the organization. The design of an information system for an evaluation system thus determines the weight that is to be given to each potential piece of information, the perception of the organization, and the definition of organizational effectiveness.

2. *Higher education institutions need information systems that reflect their unique form of governance and division of labor.* Information systems are often designed for use by managers and executives. Leaders desire information to help them plan, monitor, and control their programs. The information base is intended to aid more rational decision making. In higher education, however, governance is not hierarchial; rather, power bases are diffuse, policy making is decentralized, and compromise, negotiation, and accommodation are more frequent than autocratic decision making by a designated authority. In discus-

sing the problems of management information systems in higher education, Parker and Gardner (1978) make a convincing argument for the distinction between managing and administering. Decisions in higher education are predominantly political and responsive, as opposed to managerial or proactive. Policies in higher education are the end result of a series of negotiations among audiences, each with their own vested interests and value perspectives. The political process is central to policy making, and the administrators lack the power and prerogative to unilaterally determine the direction and policies of an institution. Those in executive positions, especially in the area of academic policy making, do not manage; rather, they administer and provide academic leadership. Parker and Gardner suggest that an information system should be designed to help different reference groups build position bases within a political environment instead of designed to help chief executives control the institution.

Thus the purpose of an information system is not for control by a chief officer, but for relevant audiences to use in an open political environment. A mechanistic bureaucratic form of governance is not the model for establishing an information system. Boland (1980) argues that designers of information systems should resist a highly centralized control system even though executives may desire one to increase their monitoring potential. An information system for an evaluation system is not intended to be used solely by the management.

The desired organizational climate and work environment of an institution of higher education also needs to be considered in designing an information system. Based on his study of human reactions to information systems, Chris Argyris (1971) concluded that a centralized, sophisticated information system creates working conditions that tend to increase manager defensiveness, conformity, and individual loss of freedom and control. In higher education, the faculty—the major service providers—can ill afford to withdraw or feel helpless about their role in the organization. Creative work and experimentation by faculty are the core of higher education, and an information system should be designed to reflect these activities.

These two features primarily relate to an information system, but an evaluation system is more than an information system. Three additional features are characteristic of an effective evaluation system.

3. *The focus of an evaluation system must be on value, worth, quality, and effectiveness.* Regardless of the multiple purposes and uses of an evaluation system, the core of an evaluation is the assessment of worth. For an academic program, worth relates to quality and effectiveness. In an evaluation of a ceramic engineering department, for example, knowledge of instructional costs for a major in ceramic engineering is necessary, but not sufficient for an evaluation of the department. Issues regarding the quality of the instructional program must also be addressed. Determining the value of a program is more than determining the instructional costs of a program. Judgments of worth and

quality are not unitary and absolute; rather, they are derived from the value perspectives of those making the judgments. Faculty, administrators, professionals, and governing boards have different perspectives about the value of a program. This diversity and pluralism of value perspectives needs to be recognized and accounted for in an evaluation system. For example, faculty may disagree with students and central administrators on the importance of faculty-student ratios and individualized research projects undertaken by senior students. An evaluation often does not resolve conflicts over value perspectives; instead, the evaluation process exposes value perspectives. A system needs to be designed so that these value perspectives can be integrated into assessments of worth and merit.

Not only do different audiences bring different value perspectives to the assessment of worth, but the mission and purpose of each institution must be taken into account in assessing the worth of a department. Quality is defined by the characteristics of the institution; that is, quality is institution specific. For example, the effectiveness of a department at a research university should not be determined in the same way as a department in an urban university with no graduate school.

4. *The communication network among the audiences should be the core of an evaluation system.* Evaluation is undertaken in a social and political environment in which various groups have vested interests in the evaluation process. The administration of academic programs and departments is based on shared authority and responsibility among faculty, administrators, and governing boards. If an evaluation is to be used by these groups in their deliberations, discussions, and policy making, the evaluation system must be designed to maximize the communication among these audiences. In designing such a system two guidelines regarding communication must be used. First, audiences and their information needs must be identified. However, pinpointing specific pieces of information to be used for specific decisions is not the goal. Rather, the intent is to establish an environment in which audiences become involved in as much of the evaluation process as possible, including making decisions about the criteria to be used in the evaluation, the data sources to be used, and interpretation and transmission of the evaluative information. Involvement may promote interest in the evaluation and increase the use of the information.

Second, the communication of information is accomplished best through open interpersonal communication channels among the various audiences—those conducting the evaluation, the faculty, and the administrators. "Effective communication . . . is not a one-way process; rather it is a dialogue which takes place over time, which allows a full sharing of concerns on both sides, and which allows for the reshaping of the message to suit the needs, concerns, and circumstances of the receiver" (Havelock, 1980, p. 12). The various audiences thus need to develop ongoing interpersonal relationships in which mutual problem solving is the goal. Trust in each other as professionals and recognition (although not necessarily agreement) of different value perspectives are more than by-products of an evaluation. Trust and acceptance are essential for interactions to be useful and for subsequent implementation of policies. Guskin (1980, p. 54) emphasizes the importance of administrators taking into account the interaction between knowledge and the people with the knowledge: "For an administrator, particularly a senior level one, knowledge relevant to a policy includes the specific substance of the issue as well as all the information that relates to the process by which the policy decision will be made and all that will enable the administration to implement it effectively. It is because of the necessity to take into account all these matters that administrators rely heavily on the informal organizational intelligence that they receive orally from their colleagues. This interaction not only enables them to receive vital information from these sources, but in doing so, they have also initiated the interpersonal process that will enable the decision to be made and implemented."

The major responsibilities of those implementing an evaluation system extend beyond collecting and transmitting information. The evaluator does not perform a set of data manipulations in isolation and then present computer printouts to designated audiences; rather, the evaluator, through developing interactive two-way communication channels among audiences, facilitates discussion. Evaluators engage audiences and users in as many phases of evaluation as possible. The users are involved in determining the data to be collected and how the data are to be interpreted. They also check and recheck the accuracy of the data and their interpretation and discuss the implications of their actions. Formal written technical reports are only part of the information flow among faculty and administrators at the local institution. Evaluators need to also recognize that users have access to multiple types of information—some informal and highly personal and political. Formal evaluative information is only one source of information, and its power depends on the dynamics of policy making within the institution.

5. *Implicit criteria and standards should be incorporated into an evaluation system.* Information available for an evaluation is selective because costs and audience needs for information are considered. The selection is also influenced by the criteria to be used in assessing program quality and effectiveness. Criteria, the bases upon which judgments of values are made, may be dimensions or characteristics of a program (for example, learning environment), outputs (scholarship), societal need for the program, or general notions of quality, efficiency, and cost effectiveness. Indicators or measures are employed to provide information about the criteria. For example, faculty publications in refereed journals can serve as an indicator of faculty scholarship of a specific department.

Not all criteria need to be explicit to be useful in the judgment of value, which may involve implicit criteria and implicit standards of excellence. For example, the value of faculty scholarship is not easily specified because it represents a configuration of faculty productivity. An overall assessment of quality of faculty research requires more than description; it requires judgments by experts and peers. The defense of a judgment may be intuitive—based on the judge's intuition, experience, and personal set of values.

In many formal evaluation systems, explicit criteria for which there are readily apparent indicators are often advocated. The tendency to rely on explicit and quantifiable data, however, can be myopic. First, if only objective measures reflecting explicit criteria are selected, the psychometric characteristics of the data are often emphasized at the expense of the credibility and relevance of the data. Credibility is the extent to which users trust the data for their use, and relevance is the extent to which the information is considered appropriate for judging quality. For example, if the administrators consider teaching loads to be irrelevant to determining program quality, there is little need to collect data on the teaching loads even though they are highly quantifiable. Given the emphasis on worth and value in an evaluation system, many types of quantitative data may be only indirectly relevant. Credibility of information should also be viewed from the perspective of the potential audiences; certain types of information may be more trustworthy than others. For example, survey data collected from students on the instructional quality of the departmental faculty or self-evaluations of teaching by the faculty may not be viewed as credible information by campus administrators or governing boards. They may only trust colleagues' observations of transactions in the classroom. Determining the relevance and credibility of information, as well as the reliability and validity of the data, is a task of those implementing the evaluation system. Determining credibility and relevance requires asking audiences for preferences for criteria and information in the evaluation. Negotiation among audiences and trade-offs between credibility and validity are often necessary.

Second, quantitative indicators and measures may not adequately represent the unique and distinguishing features and characteristics of the program being evaluated. How much error is involved in the abstracting process of summarizing data based on quantitative indices? Does the selection of only a few indicators completely portray the operation of the department and its strengths and weaknesses? For example, student credit hours produced by a department is a frequent indicator of department efficiency and may imply effectiveness. But do these data reflect teaching effort and time, quality of teaching, differing teaching modes necessitated by differences in disciplines, student demand for courses, and quality of student-teacher relationships? The inability of a single measure to represent all aspects of a program often goes unheeded; too quickly its use is defended by its explicitness rather than by its representational value. Holistic professional judgments about program quality are often preferrable, even though they may not be able to be stored in some central computer-based information system. Although information about academic quality is perhaps best reported in a form that is not easily quantified, it more accurately portrays the complexity of the program, highlights the issues and concerns of those involved, and allows for a variety of value positions to be considered in the process of evaluating a specific program. Subjective and qualitative information can be as credible as quantifiable information. Although counting the number of majors in a department can be done more reliably than assessing the quality of teaching, it does not necessarily follow that reliable data are therefore more valid, credible, relevant, and useful. Thus information not easily stored and retrieved can be among the most useful in an evaluation system.

Third, the use of only quantifiable data might unduly influence policy decisions in directions not intended or desired. For example, student credit hours is commonly used as an indicator of instructional effort and serves as a basis for resource reallocation decisions. If these hours are considered important, faculty and college administrators of units within the institution may adjust their educational programs to generate more of them. Requiring more courses within a college for a student major or discouraging and even denying electives outside the student's major or college are possible strategies, but they may run counter to the overall mission of the institution.

Fourth, if only centrally collected data as indicators of explicit criteria are used in an evaluation, some audiences may have a reduced role in the evaluation process. A centralized data system may result in less authority at the local level; for example, the role of faculty members may be reduced. Do we need common guidelines, common criteria with common data bases to judge quality? Where should the locus of power for determining effectiveness be? A decentralized approach involving faculty and peers is a more appropriate strategy for judging quality and effectiveness of academic programs than a centralized approach.

An alternative to use of explicit criteria is the use of issues (salient and important matters that need attention) and concerns (disagreements about matters by relevant constituencies) as the advanced organizers. The use of issues and concerns implies a broader view of the assessment of the department, and an evaluation that will not result in some final summative rating of the goodness or badness of the department. This use also implies a more inductive approach, since concerns and issues are allowed to emerge during the evaluation rather than forcing an *a priori* list upon the program evaluated. Problems and future aspirations unique to a program receive more attention, which may be beneficial for linking evaluation with planning.

Case Studies

Numerous evaluation systems have been developed, both at the state and institutional level (Barak and Berdahl, 1978). The two summarized below are at the institutional level and represent approaches to program evaluation.

University of Illinois System: COPE. In May 1972, the University of Illinois at Urbana-Champaign Senate adopted a recommendation from a blue-ribbon committee that a program evaluation system be established to conduct periodic in-depth reviews of all academic and administrative units. A faculty-dominated Council on Program Evaluation (COPE) was established to review every department once every five years for the purpose of improving quality and providing administrators with information for reallocation of resources. This dual purpose has stayed relatively intact but the approach used to evaluate departments has evolved considerably. The evaluation system has incorporated six major criteria: quality of instruction, scholarly works, and service; centrality; value of unit to society; and potential and future expectations (Office of Planning and Evaluation, 1980).

In 1973–74 task groups of seven to twelve faculty and one or two students were selected to conduct each in-depth review. They had access to central data files and conducted extensive interviews according to established guidelines. This approach to evaluation was so demanding of faculty time that in 1975 a new procedure was developed; it involved a departmental self-study, student and alumni surveys, faculty activity questionnaire, and collection of data from central information systems. The council reviewed this information and prepared an evaluative report. Between 1973 and 1979 the council evaluated all departments and a few administrative units on campus.

In 1980 the council initiated a second round of departmental evaluations. In the second cycle, a two-stage evaluation strategy is employed. The first stage involves an initial review of all departments on the basis of data secured from central information systems (for example, enrollments and instructional costs), faculty vitae, student and faculty survey results, and a departmental response to five open-ended questions. Judgmental and qualitative data are given considerable weight. After these data are collected, COPE staff assemble a sourcebook, which is sent to a COPE subcommittee and to each department. The subcommittee meets with the departments to discuss the sourcebook information and then reports its findings to COPE. If special problems are identified, COPE institutes more in-depth information collection procedures such as asking the department to study and report on a problem area, inviting an external review team to study specific concerns (serious discipline problems, for example), or appointing an on-campus task group to investigate areas of concern. Following discussion of all collected data, COPE formulates a set of conclusions and recommendations, which are presented to the department in draft form by the COPE subcommittee. In its final form the evaluation is sent to the department, the vice-chancellor for academic affairs, the dean of the appropriate college, and others identified in the report. Within six months, the vice-chancellor meets with the dean (and school head where appropriate) to discuss actions taken as a result of the evaluation and plans for the future.

One important characteristic of the evaluation procedure is the amount of informal dialogue between COPE members and faculty from the departments. The evaluation process is interactive; that is, COPE members and local departmental administrators and faculty are engaged in frequent person-to-person contact. Initially, there is negotiation on what information needs to be collected and on identification of major issues and problems. In the second cycle, discussion of uncovered issues and concerns between COPE and the department form much of the evaluation strategy. Followup discussions on possible actions by higher level administration is part of the process. The link between evaluation and development is stressed.

University of Nebraska-Lincoln System: Academic Program Review. At the University of Nebraska, a process was established in 1973 to identify "areas of excellence" in certain departments or colleges; special funding for these areas was requested of state government. As a part of this development, designed to improve selected programs with special state allocations, a committee was set up for each area of excellence. Each committee consisted of faculty members, both internal and external to the university, an academic administrator, a regent, a student, a state legislator, and a representative of the governor. The committee was to provide general oversight for the expenditure of the budget funds for the area of excellence and to evaluate, over a three-year period, the progress of the unit toward its agreed-on goals. Each review committee made annual visits to the university. In the first year, the committee reviewed a self-study report written by the departmental faculty and determined if the goals were realistic in relation to trends and needs. The committee assessed the extent to which program plans would lead to the desired level of excellence. After their first annual on-site visit, the external review team made recommendations for modifying the goals and the plans for achieving the goals. The goals were then solidified and were used as benchmarks by the committee in assessing progress. The second-year review was still primarily formative whereas the third-year review was both formative and summative.

To assess progress of selected academic programs, this evaluation system was to provide a process for assessing quality, to improve the credibility of the university by establishing direct communication between the university and state government, and to improve both short- and long-term planning by supplying local staff with systematic feedback over a three-year period.

In 1978, the Academic Planning Committee (APC), a faculty-dominated campuswide committee, prepared a set of guidelines for the evaluation of all instructional and noninstructional programs on a five-year cycle. Added attention was given to long-range planning. Initially, each program conducts a self-study describing program goals, rationale, program offerings, staffing, resources, students, and strategies for improvement. Next, the review team, consisting of peers in similar disciplines from other universities, as well as students, alumni, campus faculty (including those from programs being evaluated), and members of the APC, are to consider the status and function of the program within UNL as well as assess program quality. The review team holds two interviews once the evaluation has been completed. One informs the program's representatives about strengths, weaknesses, and potential opportunities. The other advises the campus administration about a preliminary evaluation.

Considerable interchange among the dean, program chairperson, and the APC is built into the process. The department and dean have opportunities to react to the review team's report, and the reactions are considered by the APC before recommendations are made to the chancellor. The report is used for budgetary decisions and helps fulfill the annual reporting requirement. The degree of progress toward the achievement of the five-year program objectives is included in the report.

Conclusion

An evaluation system that contains the five features listed in this chapter is dynamic, highly interactive, and localized for each institution. Information used in the formal evaluation process partially determines the social reality of the institution. Not all information in an evaluation needs to be quantifiable and stored in a central computer file. On the contrary, an evaluation system should reflect a decentralized and diffuse nature of policy making especially that involving academic programs. Continual involvement of various audiences in the evaluation process is needed to obtain their value perspectives and to establish a mutual problem-solving, trusting relationship, a condition that also facilitates subsequent policy making, program planning, and program implementation.

The two systems described here have incorporated these five features, although they are different. The credibility of the evaluation systems was given considerable attention in both designs. In the areas of excellence evaluation at Nebraska, an academic and budget planning system, written by representatives of the faculty and the legislative fiscal office staff, was formally accepted by the board of regents of the university and the state legislature as the review and planning procedure to be employed. The latest cyclical review system was included in the university by-laws, which received extensive review from several constituencies before the final version was adopted by the regents. At Illinois, a prestigious committee recommended the formation of the review system and received the faculty senate's approval before its implementation.

The extent to which these systems reflect the desired social reality depends on the use made of the system. At Nebraska, the evaluations for areas of excellence were highly visible, but their value was questioned by some faculty. Is such a close scrutiny necessary for the amount of additional funds allocated? High visibility and special attention also made the departments more aware of their need to demonstrate accountability to the state government regardless of the extent to which the formal evaluation was useful to the local departments. There was also some concern that the new reporting requirements altered the existing administrative and policy-making structure, and the departments being evaluated enjoyed a special and unwarranted status in the higher levels of campus administration. In the revision at Nebraska, the membership of the evaluation committee has been reduced to those in academe, and the lines of internal communication are spelled out. In the early years at Illinois, considerable debate over the usefulness of the evaluation occurred because dramatic decisions about programs were linked to evaluations. In more recent years, visibility has subsided. Thus the influence of an evaluation on the governance of the institution is less. The seriousness that audiences, especially faculty, give to an evaluation seems to be related to the estimated pay-off of the evaluation; that is, if the evaluation does not lead to allocation decisions, the evaluation is less of a threat and intrusion to those potentially influenced by the evaluation.

Both evaluation systems have an extensive communication network among audiences. The network at Nebraska was more inclusive since representatives from the regents and state government were key members of the review team. This arrangement had considerable symbolic as well as practical significance. Public officials as well as professionals were actively engaged in assessing effectiveness. By implication, public officials outside academe were given the right to judge academic quality. As a communication device, the scheme worked quite well, despite the faculty's original skepticism. Those outside the university who participated learned a good deal and generally their views of the university improved. Faculty members found that regents, legislators, and students who were meaningfully involved over a period of time made valuable suggestions for department planning and evaluation.

In both systems, the discussion about the data is interactive. Provisions are built in so that departments and evaluative committees react to each other. Differences of interpretation of the data become part of the information used in the entire process. Increased understanding by potential audiences is one of the major purposes of these systems. The systems are also designed to lead to action. Those responsible for budget decisions—vice-chancellors and chancellors, for example, have follow-up meetings with deans to discuss progress. The integration between evaluation and development is recognized, although the linkage appears more informal than formal, especially at Illinois.

The two evaluation systems are more than information systems because of the emphasis placed on judgment of value and quality relative to description of program output. Descriptive information is used but so are judgments. Data from central files have been used continuously at both institutions, but other information has been collected. At the University of Illinois, judgment data (student majors' perceptions of the instructional quality of the department and faculty perceptions of departmental governance and quality of research, teaching, and service) are crucial. At the University of Nebraska, judgment data are also a key ingredient, but they stem from a different source. At Illinois, the faculty and students provide the major judgments of quality, whereas at Nebraska, the review team, which consists of alumni and peers from other institutions, provides the crucial judgment data.

The ultimate defense of any evaluation system is its utility, that is, to what extent is the expenditure of time and financial resources improving the institution? The impact of an evaluation system is difficult to assess, but three minimal requirements for an effective system are necessary. First, the evaluation system reinforces the desired character of the institution. The governance of an institution must be incorporated into the design of an evaluation system. Second, those who use the information are more enlightened, more aware of strengths and weaknesses, and more cognizant of the political, economic, and contextual constraints of programs being evaluated. And finally, the evaluation system is viewed as fair. If these three conditions are not met, then the evaluation system may not be worth it.

References

Academic Planning Committee. *Academic Program Review Guidelines.* Lincoln: University of Nebraska, October 1978.

Argyris, C. "Management Information Systems: The Challenge to Rationality and Emotionality." *Management Science,* 1971, *17* (6), 275–292.

Barak, R. J., and Berdahl, R. O. *State Level Academic Program Review in Higher Education.* Report No. 107. Denver: Education Commission of the States, February 1978.

Boland, R. J. "Some Ethical Considerations in Designing an Organization's Information System." Faculty Working Paper No. 697. Urbana: College of Commerce and Business Administration, University of Illinois, 1980.

Clark, M. J. *Program Review Practices of University Departments.* The Graduate Record Examinations Board Research Report GREB No. 75-5aR. Princeton, N.J.: Educational Testing Service, July 1977.

Guskin, A. E. "Knowledge Utilization and Power in University Decision Making." In L. A. Braskamp and R. D. Brown (Eds.), *New Directions for Program Evaluation: Utilization of Evaluative Information,* no. 5. San Francisco: Jossey-Bass, 1980.

Havelock, R. G. "Forward." In J. Rothman, *Using Research in Organizations.* Beverly Hills, Calif.: Sage, 1980.

Office of Planning and Evaluation. *Council on Program Evaluation: Second Cycle Evaluation Procedure.* Unpublished manuscript, University of Illinois, 1980.

Parker, J. D., and Gardner, D. E. "Information Will Not Make You Well: MIS Re-Examined." Paper presented at annual convention of the Association of Institutional Research, Houston, May 1978.

Patrick, C., and Caruthers, J. K. "Management Priorities of College Presidents." *Research in Higher Education,* 1980, *12* (3), 195–214.

Van de Ven, A. H., and Ferry, D. L. *Measuring and Assessing Organizations.* New York: Wiley, 1980.

Larry A. Braskamp is professor of educational psychology and head of the Measurement and Research Division of the Office of Instructional Resources at the University of Illinois at Urbana-Champaign.

The network of people that decides what questions to ask, that interprets and judges the information, and that is expected to use the results must be an important consideration in any evaluation plan.

Planning for an Evaluation Network and Institutionalization

H. Richard Smock

In the context of this chapter, *program evaluation* is an organized process of collecting and disseminating information to assist administrators and faculty in making judgments about the value of academic departments and programs. An important assumption of the definition is that, while evaluation results may influence the decision-making process, the results themselves produce judgments—not decisions. Whether or not the judgments lead directly to decisions or are linked to the decision-making process in a more indirect and less observable manner depends more upon the network of people designed to implement the system of program evaluation than on the evaluation results themselves.

Adaptive Systems and Responsive Evaluation

In Chapter Two Petrie warned us that frustration will result if the organization and the proposed evaluation program are not understood as interactive systems. Thinking about organizations and program evaluations as interactive adaptive systems has an implication that counters the idea of being able to offer exact models or precise prescriptions for planning and developing an internal evaluation system. The implication is that the planning process

R. Wilson (Ed.). *New Directions for Higher Education: Designing Academic Program Reviews,* no. 37. San Francisco: Jossey-Bass, March 1982.

itself, as well as the evaluation design, must adapt to the organization in several ways unique to each college or university, such as the degree of administrative or faculty control, the extent of unionization, the interaction of various power groups on campus, or even the personality of particular leaders. Evaluation models suitable for the evaluation of research universities cannot be simply scaled-down to serve the needs of a community college. A cyclical institutionalized system adds an additional demand for adaptive planning because a previous evaluation becomes part of the organizational context for the next cycle, and adaptive planning requires that the system respond to the unique environmental factors at each institution. In other words, I am advocating planning for a moving target. Evaluation plans predicated on static models or assumed for static organizations can quickly become another bureaucratic requirement rather than a vital and important activity in the life of a campus.

Planning an evaluation based on interactive and adaptive concepts requires an evaluation plan that is sensitive to changing conditions. Responsive evaluation, as conceptualized and extensively discussed by Stake (1975), provides an evaluation approach to meet that requirement, and it is the approach assumed here. In his terms, an evaluation plan is responsive "If it orients more directly to program activities than to program intents, responds to audience requirements for information, and if the different value perspectives present are referred to in reporting the success and failure of the program" (p. 14). An evaluation plan that seeks to discover purposes and concerns and that focuses on present program issues or on issues related to value perspectives of various audiences seems best suited to the nature of campus evaluation systems.

Developing a Program Evaluation Plan

Figure 1 provides a conceptualization of key elements in a program evaluation plan. After assuming that there is a purpose for developing an eval-

Figure 1. Factors to Consider in Planning for Program Evaluation

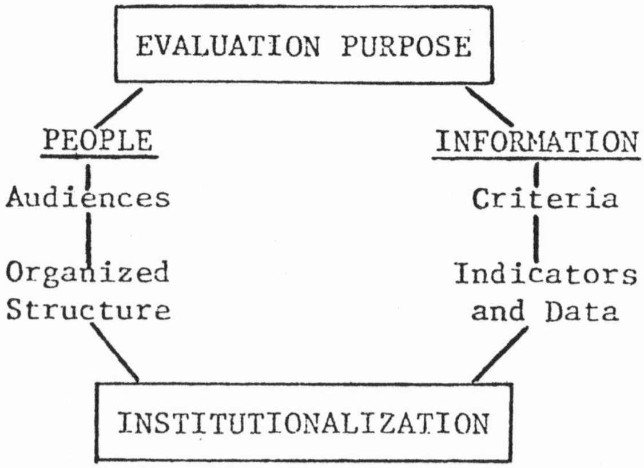

uation plan, one moves neither from left to right nor from top to bottom but in a linear fashion. Although the list has some logical order, the topics are not discrete and questions relating to one cannot be answered before taking up another.

Because evaluation purposes, criteria, and indicators are discussed at length elsewhere in this sourcebook, I will focus on the other major dimensions, namely the network of people that guide the evaluation system, collect and interpret information, and consider evaluation results and the factors to consider if the program evaluation system is to be institutionalized as a continuing process. It is becoming common for colleges and universities to plan for cyclical or continuing processes of program evaluation.

Planning for the Network of People

Although the give and take of the planning process requires concurrent consideration of many matters, one of the most important is the network of people including those in the evaluated unit or program, those who decide what questions to ask and what to measure, those considering and interpreting information, and those who are expected to act on the results. The effectiveness of this network will have more impact on the utility of the results than will the information assembled as part of the evaluation. The planning process that does not give full consideration to the network is neglecting an essential component of an evaluation system. Good sources of wisdom for planning the network are administrators, faculty, and perhaps students—the people most intimately involved in the life of the campus—as well as evaluators who recognize the need for this planning.

Let us now look at the factors to be considered in designing the human network structure.

Audiences. Evaluation audiences are individuals or identifiable groups of people who have a special stake or legitimate interests in the evaluation results. Early in the planning process, responsive program evaluators consider the information needs of audiences to be served because these needs affect other aspects of planning (Stake, 1975). Procedures for informing different audiences, the nature of the information that will be most useful to them, and the degree to which they will be involved in the evaluation process itself are all subject to planning.

Although most evaluations are of interest to a number of audiences, planners can think of audiences as groups that represent the evaluated program or department, those that interpret and form judgments as part of the evaluation process, and those expected to act on the resulting judgments. In addition there are often audiences of a more general nature, such as others in the academic community or state legislators, that have some valid interest in the academic enterprise. Different audiences require different forms of communication and interpretation, and the degree of confidentiality, anonymity, and specificity in communicating with them will vary depending upon the legitimate audience needs. Some audiences such as those representing evaluated departments or programs may have a legitimate claim to a voice in the planning and implementation of an evaluation system. Other audiences are logically more passive observers who nevertheless may reasonably expect to be kept informed.

How each of the audiences is to be advised about the progress and results of program evaluation is determined through the planning process. Evaluations that are carried out as publicly as possible can help inhibit the spread of rumors and the appearance of a campus evaluation as more of an investigative, rather than an academic, endeavor. Keeping important audiences fully apprised of progress can also help in establishing credibility. However, keeping audiences appropriately informed, informally or formally, orally or in writing, can be an expensive and time-consuming process that can slow down the evaluation effort.

Organizing the Structure. Evaluations can be powerful inducements for change or relatively ineffectual, depending on the organization of the network through which the evaluative information will be collected, considered, and acted upon. Not only is it a matter of how the network is structured, but also who is selected to be part of it. Democratically elected committees will behave differently than appointed or voluntary committees. Recommendations from a body composed of academic heavyweights will be different than those coming from more broadly representative bodies. While reliability and validity are yardsticks of quality that can be applied to data, trust and fairness are similar yardsticks by which to judge the structure. Program evaluation systems that are sensitive to the power arrangements on campus, aware that there can seldom be too much communication, and designed so that sound judgments are forthcoming are likely to measure high on the trust and fairness yardsticks. After all, judgment is at the heart of evaluation, and there is a question of credibility in all judgments. The degree of credibility of the process will depend on the interaction of particular audiences with particular people and structures. These factors signal the amount of attention that ought to be paid to planning the structure. Planning decisions related to setting up an organization include those related to assignment of staff responsible for designing and implementing the program evaluation, to determination of the selection process and the audiences to be represented in the membership of evaluative committees, and to design of the linkage to the administrative process.

Since the evaluation method will affect the shape of the stucture, planners should devote time and care to its selection. The more common evaluation methods, such as peer review, independent external evaluations, task group evaluations, and self-studies are discussed elsewhere in this sourcebook. In addition, House, in Chapter One, provides valuable insight into a variety of evaluation strategies such as the systems approach, the behavioral objectives approach, and the case study approach that may be adapted to the method selected.

If program evaluation results are intended to be used, then an organizational structure that is capable and likely to use them must be planned. The structure will need to accommodate such questions as who interprets and makes judgments about the data, how and through what channels will the judgments be communicated, and what assurances are there that the results will have a high utility value?

One of the current concerns of program evaluators is the lack of impact of evaluation results (Braskamp and Brown, 1980). Guskin (1980) is of the opinion that past analyses of how administrators process information tend to overemphasize the role of administrators as decision makers. He says that "information gets utilized in university decision-making councils and, therefore, by presidents, within the context of very elaborate organizational, interpersonal, and psychological processes. Focusing on the person and the role of the leader as the sole decision maker misses the dynamics of university decision making and neglects the real influence (rather than authority) of chief executives to exercise and/or to redirect significant impact on the universities they lead" (p. 46). This viewpoint reinforces the interactive nature of program evaluation and the organization and places the importance of the network that handles matters related to the interpretation, communication, and utilization of evaluative information in its proper perspective.

The options for planners are many and are best considered in the context of a particular academic setting. They range from systems in which the information-gathering activities are completely separated from considerations of data interpretation, communication, and utilization, to those in which integration is complete. A task group, for an example of one possible combination of these variables, may be charged with obtaining information about a program through interviews and observations based on criteria determined by a separate committee, combining that information with data from an Office of Institutional Reserach, and interpreting the results. It could be asked to direct recommendations to an administrator responsible for action, or it could forward its results to a committee of faculty, which reinterprets the recommendations from task groups examining similar departments or programs. In turn, that committee could pass on their recommendations to appropriate administrators. In addition to these possible arrangements, at each step choices must be made related to the degree of confidentiality to be maintained, whether or not information is given in written or oral form, and what information will be made available to the evaluated unit and other audiences.

Institutionalization of Program Evaluation Systems

Cyclical program evaluations are a long-range commitment. Because program evaluation and the institutions in which they operate are interactive, the campus climate that exists at the end of the first cycle is apt to point up problems that need to be handled differently during the next cycle.

Evaluations undertaken with the purpose of serving program improvement or resource allocation carry the expectation of change, but most administrators and faculty who have had experience with attempts to make substantive change in any aspects of higher education know how difficult change is to accomplish. The academic establishment, including tenured faculty, is characterized by considerable career stability and will tolerate only a modest and carefully paced rate of change. Program evaluation systems that press to accelerate the rate of change can be expected to have an unsettling effect (Smith, 1980). In addition we lack knowledge about how to use negative information to produce positive change, and evaluation for improvement often must criticize if it is to serve its purpose. However, criticism can produce defensive reactions as often as change. Program evaluations that fail to cope satisfactorily with the rate of change (either too fast or too slow) and with the problem of using negative information positively can raise tensions on campus to a point where institutionalization of the evaluation system could be counterproductive. The overall impact of the system may be altered for successive cycles, depending upon the conditions prevailing on campus.

Evaluation impact can be measured in two ways. One is the amount of change that occurs through the administrative decision-making process as a result of the evaluation. The other is the amount of change induced through the educational impact the program evaluation system has on faculty and administrators. The relationship between change related to the decision process and evaluation impact may be either direct or indirect. Although many evaluation critics have expressed concern that program evaluations are not publicly and directly linked to immediate decisions, a less-direct relationship between results and decisions—one buffered by the normal political and administrative mechanisms of the campus and tempered by intervals that avoid direct confrontation—may be more in keeping with the organizational style found in higher education and thus more effective, as well as humane, in the long run. For example, after a negative evaluation a department head could be given some time to review career goals in the hope that a decision to return to the classroom and scholarly pursuits will be made.

The educational purposes served by program evaluation, that is, the ability of program evaluation systems to transmit to a campus the norms and expectations of particular groups through the criteria they employ, the questions they ask, and the standards they apply, can exert a powerful influence on departments and programs. Change in desired directions can result even in departments and programs not directly evaluated, especially when the campus is aware that the evaluations will be cyclical. The evaluation process is an excellent vehicle for disseminating the educational values and expectations of the campus.

The on-campus visibility of the program evaluation system is another factor that is linked to impact, whether measured by the change produced or the educational results. Visibility can be conceptually separated from impact;

systems with high campus visibility may have either high or low impact, or systems with low visibility can be coupled to either high or low impact. A high visibility system with high impact would involve many people operating in an open communication network with the results immediately affecting resource allocation. A low visibility system with high impact might be one in which a dean is empowered to interview program directors and make immediate changes as he or she determines.

Time is a factor that can mask the relationship between visibility and impact. Immediate change is clearly of high impact, but the same results could be achieved over a longer period of time; even though the impact would not be apparent immediately. The use of time as a buffer is a device that can insure humaneness in the evaluation system.

Each of the factors of impact, visibility, and time is amenable in some degree to planning, and each will affect the success or failure of the evaluation effort. Furthermore, in institutionalized systems it may be desirable to alter any of these dimensions, depending on the conditions found on campus at a particular time.

References

Braskamp, L. A., and Brown, R. D. (Eds.). *New Directions for Program Evaluation: Utilization of Evaluative Information*, no. 5. San Francisco: Jossey-Bass, 1980.

Guskin, A. E. "Knowledge Utilization and Power in University Decision Making." In L. A. Braskamp and R. D. Brown (Eds.), *New Directions for Program Evaluation: Utilization of Evaluative Information,* no. 5. San Francisco: Jossey-Bass, 1980.

Smith, D. K. "Multi-Campus System Approaches to Acadmic Program Evaluation." In E. C. Craven (Ed.), *New Direction for Institutional Research: Academic Program Evaluation,* no. 27. San Francisco: Jossey-Bass, 1980.

Stake, R. E. "To Evaluate an Art Program." In R. Stake (Ed.), *Evaluating the Arts in Education: A Responsive Approach.* Columbus, Ohio: Merrill, 1975.

H. Richard Smock is head of the Course Development Division in the office of Instructional Resources at the University of Illinois at Urbana-Champaign.

Differences in state-level program review processes can be explained in terms of six key design decisions and the implementation environment.

Process Issues in State-Level Program Reviews

Robert A. Wallhaus

There are several determinations that must be made in designing any program review process. These decisions, which will characterize the program review process and ultimately determine its acceptance and effectiveness, include:

1. Determining the purposes and objectives of program review,
2. Determining and defining the scope and focus of the program review,
3. Determining the schedule and timing of program reviews,
4. Determining criteria to be used in program assessment and how to support the application of such criteria,
5. Determining who will be involved in program review and their roles and responsibilities,
6. Determining what decisions will be made as a result of program review.

The major differences among program review processes utilized in different states are related to how these issues are resolved. In each case there are various alternatives; each alternative will offer certain advantages and disadvantages depending largely upon factors related to the environment in which they are to be implemented (for example, the statutory authorities of the state postsecondary education agency in relation to various campuses and sectors of

R. Wilson (Ed.). *New Directions for Higher Education: Designing Academic Program Reviews,* no. 37.
San Francisco: Jossey-Bass, March 1982.

higher education). Craven (1980) analyses the full scope of issues that arise in designing program evaluations, and, in a section entitled "Conducting an Evaluation" (pp. 444–449), he proposes a series of questions that must be answered in designing and implementing an effective evaluation. Barak and Berdahl (1978) study the different approaches to program review that are utilized by different state agencies across the country, and Engdahl and Barak (1980) report the results of a survey and analysis of program reviews carried out in the thirteen western states that are included in the Western Interstate Commission for Higher Education (WICHE) compact.

This chapter identifies the possible choices in each of the six areas just identified and analyzes the pros and cons associated with these alternatives. Particular attention in this analysis is given to the relationship between state- and institutional-level program reviews.

Determining the Purposes of Program Review

The definition of purposes is logically the first step in developing a program review process, and yet it is a step that is frequently never clarified. Often this lack of clarity reflects an unwillingness to face the reality that a well-conceived examination will result in conclusions—some good, but some bad, at least from certain perspectives. On the other hand, leaving purposes and objectives undefined can result in distrust and, in the extreme, manipulation of the process and its outcomes.

Table 1 displays a range of purposes and objectives for program review. Although no single program review could serve all of these purposes, most program reviews are designed to serve multiple objectives. Certain purposes and objectives are relevant to the responsibilities of state agencies, while others are more closely tied to decisions that are made by governing boards, campuses, or academic units within an institution. Table 1 classifies these purposes and objectives according to whether they are primarily related to institutional, as opposed to state-level, decisions and responsibilities to show areas of overlap and potential conflict. However, considerable variations along this continuum occur according to such factors as state agency statutory authorities, type of institution (for example, public or private), academic environment (selective versus "open door"), and governance structures (local versus statewide board of control). Chance (1980) analyzes the purposes of program review that are appropriate to state-level agencies and discusses how these can be complementary to purposes at the institutional level. Those purposes and objectives outlined in Table 1 with state-level implications are discussed briefly here.

Statewide Educational Policies and Plans. It is impossible to examine statewide educational policies, long-range plans or programmatic priorities on the basis of independent reviews of individual programs. At the same time one must recognize that individual programs are the building blocks that, taken

Table 1. Purposes and Objectives of Program Review

	Tends to be more closely tied to state-level responsibilities ←			*Tends to be more closely tied to institutional responsibilities* →
A. Determination of statewide educational policies, long-range plans, and programmatic priorities (that is, support development of statewide master plans)	X			
B. Elimination of unnecessary program duplication, or, conversely, identification of needs for new programs		X		
C. Determination of educational and economic priorities in terms of: consistency with role and mission			X	
need for improvement or expansion and additional resources necessary to accomplish (linkage to budget decisions)			X	
decisions to decrease or terminate (linkage to resource reallocation decisions)			X	
D. Determination of relationship to established standards of quality, or preparation for entry into professions, and so on (linkage to accreditation, continuation of operating authority or licensing authority)			X	
E. Improving communications with constituents; assuring information provided to students and prospective students, parents, alumni, governmental agencies, and others is consistent with actual practice			X	
F. Determination of quality controls and policies (for example, admission policy, graduation requirements)				X
G. Determination of curricular modifications, advisement procedures, institutional plans and priorities relative to instructional, research, and service objectives				X
H. Personnel and organizational decisions—faculty promotion and tenure, academic leadership, organizational structures, and philosophies				X

collectively and properly integrated, serve to define a statewide master plan. Thus, an assessment across the board of the strengths and weaknesses of existing programs and the future plans and priorities for program development become the basis for accomplishing this purpose of program review. Such reviews are usually initiated by the coordinating or governing board for higher education in the state, but should include all sectors of higher education in the design, collection of data, interpretation of results, and formulation of policy and plans. Often it is desirable to facilitate statewide planning purposes by focusing on an academic discipline or group of related disciplines (for example, all programs for education in the health professions) or selected functions, such as research or continuing education. It is particularly important to establish criteria and to seek information that extend beyond the individual programs in the academic area being studied. For example, national trends in student demand and projected statewide and national employment opportunities should be considered.

Statewide Program Mix. Program duplication, or the need for additional programs, cannot be considered from the perspective of isolated individual program by program reviews. But, the capability of existing programs to handle projected student interests and job market demands, the possibility of expanding existing programs without impairing their quality, and the appropriate distribution of programs geographically, by sector, and by institutional mission—serving a local, regional, or in-service clientele, for example, are certainly factors to consider in determining the proper programmatic mix from a statewide perspective. These insights can be partially derived from individual program reviews.

Educational and Economic Justification. The greatest potential for conflict between state agencies and institutions arises when the purpose of program review centers on the determination of educational and economic priorities. First, this question is usually relevant to state agencies responsible for planning and budgeting and is certainly relevant to budget decisions of campus-level administrations, as well as each level of academic unit within the campus. In other words, there is considerable overlap in responsibilities with regard to this purpose of program review, and questions of turf will surely be raised. Second, this is a double-edged purpose. When programmatic deficiencies are found, the deficiency can be corrected, which usually requires additional resources—a good outcome for the campus directly involved, or the program can be eliminated. Given these risks and uncertainties, some people would rather avoid the assessment altogether.

Although state agencies have responsibilities and interests in such areas as establishing quality standards, preparing for entry into professions, improving communications with constituents, and the other purposes for program review identified in Table 1, the driving force for these purposes runs more in the direction of institutional responsibilities. Nevertheless, in designing a state-level program review, one should recognize that the purposes of program review are not unidimensional. These purposes overlap, and if properly conceived, can be mutually supportive.

Determining and Defining the Scope and Focus of the Program Review Process

The general thrust of program review, that is, an assessment of strengths and weaknesses, is equally applicable to nonacademic areas as it is to research, public service, and instruction. Theoretically, a program review process could be designed to encompass academic as well as support areas. However, differences in objectives and definitions of productivity between instructional programs and support programs are considerable and would preclude the possibility of a single grand design for program review. Program reviews cannot ignore the nonacademic areas, which typically account for approximately 40 percent of total institutional expenditures. However, the key issues for administrative and support functions center on operational efficiencies and management and personnel concerns, and it is very difficult to define an appropriate state-level role in this context. For this reason, most state agencies have focused their program review efforts on academic programs.

However, difficulties also arise in defining the scope and focus of program reviews in the academic areas. On the one hand, there is a close relationship between the research, instruction, and public service that is carried out in a given discipline. On the other hand, there are considerable differences in objectives and clientele served by research, public service, and instructional programs. A program review designed to examine statewide planning and policy issues related to research (that is, purpose A in Table 1) would focus on such questions as the appropriate mix of state support relative to external funds, the extent to which research enterprise and resources in colleges and universities are congruent with the problem-solving priorities of the state's industry and social agencies, and the delineation of institutional research missions. But a different set of issues would be raised at the institutional level, including questions concerning the critical mass of resources, such as faculty interests and expertise, that is necessary to advance knowledge at the leading edge of the discipline or compete effectively in the arena of national research priorities. Consequently, it is difficult to build upon institutional level reviews of research and public service programs to accomplish state-level purposes. Thus, most state-level studies related to research and public service have been conceptualized as a unique effort to examine a particular policy issue.

A key question in designing state-level review processes for instructional programs is whether the focus should be on degree programs, or on disciplines or organizational units, such as academic departments or colleges). Student objectives, as well as those related to societal concerns and occupational opportunities, are closely aligned with degree programs. This perspective is consequently more compatible with state-level interests in program review as defined in Table 1. It is virtually impossible, however, to separate certain fundamental programmatic characteristics by degree program. For example, it is unrealistic to delineate particular faculty activities by degree level. Furthermore, purposes related to determination of admissions policy and graduation requirements, curriculum, and personnel and organizational decisions that are of primary interest to the campus and academic units are more closely aligned with a discipline structure. (See items F, G, and H in Table 1.) Consequently, the discipline or organizational unit perspective is most compatible with institutional objectives related to program review. This definitional incompatibility between state-level and institutional-level perspectives becomes particularly pronounced in the area of greatest overlap in purpose—namely, with regard to establishing educational and economic priorities (purpose C in Table 1). The usual compromise is to review concurrently all degree programs within a given discipline. This permits various purposes to be served simultaneously and alleviates data development problems.

Some states have chosen to focus their program review activities on a particular level of instruction; for example, they may review all doctoral programs within a specific time. This decision is undoubtedly driven by a preconception of where the major problems lie with program quality, unnecessary duplication, or ineffective use of resources. Structurally, this definition of the scope and focus of program review creates many of the definitional difficulties already identified, such as the problem of determining the resources, activities, and objectives that are neatly aligned with doctoral offerings, as opposed to other degrees within a given discipline. In addition, because the implied thrust is to deal with certain preconceived problems, this definition of scope is likely to meet considerable resistance.

Determining the Schedule and Timing of Program Reviews

The question of when program reviews should be carried out is, of course, closely tied to the question of the focus and scope of program review discussed in the preceding section. Aside from the obvious advantages of attenuating the faculty and staff effort that is involved in program review, there are other good reasons to structure program review as a systematic, continuous process as opposed to a one-shot, grand-scale effort to be carried out over one or two years. Momentum is hard to achieve, given the complexity of most program reviews. In addition, there are many questions and concerns with regard to purpose, criteria, and procedure, and these must be addressed. Considerable time and commitment is required to implement a process for program review, and it makes little sense to periodically dismantle and then reconstruct the process again at a later time.

Table 2 identifies several alternatives for scheduling program reviews and briefly comments on the advantages and disadvantages of each. Obvi-

Table 2. Alternatives for Scheduling Program Reviews

	Advantages	*Disadvantages*
A. All programs reviewed on a cyclical basis (for example, once every five years)	Assures all programs are periodically examined Easier to organize and manage; allows units to systematically prepare for reviews; Smooths workload at campus and state levels	Potential for redundant or wasted effort (that is, the process is carried out whether it is warranted or not)
B. Schedules meshed with external requirements (for example, accreditation reviews)	Eliminates redundancy, which is inevitable if this is not done	Internal purposes may be driven by external requirements and hence not realized to fullest possible extent
C. Selection based on key indicators (for example, enrollment or resource trends)	Serves to focus review efforts in areas where program modifications may be necessary	Raises concerns relative to the unreliability of the indicators, which may not be sufficiently sensitive or applicable to avoid triggering "unwarranted" reviews Does not ensure that all programs will be examined even over long periods of time Usually carries negative connotations; indicators point to problems
D. Crisis selection (for example, reviews based on student complaints or concerns raised by state agency or other institutions relative to unnecessary program duplication)	Focus of program review is on problem areas and needed modifications	Reviews driven largely by negative factors, most of which may be external to program Crisis management, the problem may be too large to address positively if uncovered too late
E. Selection based on policy or planning rationale related to certain categories of programs (by instructional level or by discipline, for example)	Facilitates comparative analyses, particularly from a state perspective Serves to more clearly delineate purposes of review	Driven largely by needs external to institutions (purpose more closely aligned with state-level interest—see Table 1). Institutional purposes may be submerged or institutional scheduling disrupted

ously, various combinations of these alternatives could be employed. For example, all programs could be scheduled initially for cyclical review, say over a five year period (Alternative A). But during the second cycle only those programs falling outside certain trigger parameters based on key indicators would be reexamined (Alternative C). Perhaps during a third cycle all programs would again be scheduled for review.

A state agency cannot examine in depth all programs in the state over any reasonable time period. Therefore, some form of "management by exception" approach is needed, particularly for the large number of community college programs in those states with extensive community college systems. Although various alternatives in Table 2 are designed to screen out a more limited number of programs for special attention, an approach based on successive iterations of great depth and detail may have considerable utility at the level of the state system or the central campus administration. For example, Illinois public universities review instructional programs on a cyclical basis. A synopsis of one to two pages, which focuses on the conclusions and recommendations resulting from the annual program reviews is transmitted to the Illinois Board of Higher Education, rather than sending the entire set of review materials and voluminous data collected during the course of the review. The Board of Higher Education staff examines these conclusions and recommendations in conjunction with basic program data on such topics as enrollment trends and cost study analyses; in the case of certain programs, the board identifies concerns or questions that they feel should be pursued further. Perhaps 90 percent of the program review synopses are accepted with no further examination deemed necessary. The general nature of the questions and concerns that are of interest to the board have been previously communicated to the universities, along with suggested data that would be responsive to these questions. Based on their in-depth review the universities submit additional information in response to the board staff's requests. Several, successively more detailed iterations, may be pursued prior to the formulation of staff recommendations that are ultimately presented to the Board of Higher Education. Thus, program review schedules can be designed around the concept of selective examination, both in terms of the number of programs reviewed as well as in terms of the depth of review that is deemed appropriate. Groves (1979) presents an historical account of how this process of state-level program review evolved in Illinois, how various difficulties were overcome, and the reasons for the number of false starts that occurred over a decade as the state-level review process was being designed and negotiated.

In summary, the scheduling of program reviews involves a consideration of a number of trade-offs: (1) frequency of program reviews versus workload requirements, (2) flexibility to respond to various purposes and external audiences versus the need to systematically organize and effectively manage the program review, and (3) rigor and depth of review versus demands on the faculty and staff at all levels.

Determining Criteria to be Used in Program Assessment and How to Support the Application of Such Criteria

Purpose, criteria, and data can be thought of as tumbling dominoes: Without well-defined purposes for program review, it is impossible to specify, communicate, or gain acceptance of the criteria that will be utilized as the basis for evaluation. And, without criteria it is impossible to define what data should be assembled, since the purpose of collecting information during a program review is to enable judgments to be made along specified dimensions.

Unfortunately, the dominoes often fall backward during the design of many program reviews. First, an attempt is made to determine what data are available. Then, there may be some consideration of what these data might mean. Finally, an attempt is made to tie this usually faulty interpretation to decisions related to the future development of the program. As a result of this approach, the program review design does not fully capitalize on the opportunities to have a valid impact on decision-making processes. Hence, no decisions result and program review is an expensive but ineffective exercise. Or, even worse, decisions are misled because the criteria utilized are inappropriate or the information examined leads to misinterpretations.

There are no set rules for establishing criteria for program reviews, but there are many trade-offs and issues that need to be considered. Table 3 addresses the extremes of those issues. The truth lies somewhere between these end points and must be determined through carefuly study, conceptualization, and negotiation. Barak and Berdahl (1978) identify program review criteria that are utilized in different states.

Determining Who Will Be Involved in the Program Review and Their Roles and Responsibilities

In designing an effective program review, some crucial questions that must be answered are who is to be involved and what will be the roles and responsibilities of these individuals? These questions are extremely difficult to answer because a number of organizational objectives are in potential conflict and sensitive balances must be achieved. That is, accomplishing certain objectives related to roles and responsibilities may well compromise others. This can be demonstrated by outlining some of the characteristics that would ideally be built into the organizational structure of program review.

Expertise. The objective is to involve in the process to the furthest extent possible those individuals with the greatest expertise and insights relative to the program or discipline being reviewed. Since program reviews address an array of different questions, they will frequently need to draw upon insights, expertise, and perspectives from a number of different quarters. This is one reason that the organizational structure for program review is often complex and seemingly involves a cast of thousands. Although these organiza-

Table 3. Considerations in Developing Criteria as a Basis for Program Evaluation

On the One Hand	*On the Other Hand*
Criteria need to be defined with as much specificity as possible (for example, a quantitative minimum number of enrollments or awards granted) if they are to be understood and applied.	Criteria for program evaluation must be established with flexibility because of the significant differences in mission, programmatic objectives, clientele served by the program, and so on.
Criteria need to be pragmatic—if quantitative data cannot be obtained relative to a criterion it should be discarded because it cannot be evaluated objectively.	Criteria need to be established to reflect the character and objectives of the program even though it will be difficult or impossible to evaluate them quantitatively. Considerable room for judgment, and subjectivity is appropriate.
Criteria ultimately will need to be determined by administrative fiat, or the review process will never get underway.	Criteria should result from consensus among all who are involved in or affected by the program review results or, at minimum, should be established by the individuals most directly associated with the program—the program faculty.
Criteria can be established in one broad conceptualization and applied to all institutions or programs. To do otherwise will preclude any comparative analyses, will create strawmen, and will consume more energy than is warranted.	Criteria must be tailored, otherwise serious misinterpretations will result and will mislead any decisions based on the program review conclusions.

tional configurations can be burdensome, this is usually a smaller price to pay than that of reaching invalid or unacceptable conclusions because the best available expertise and understanding was not utilized at the appropriate points in the review. (A more in-depth discussion of this topic is presented by House in his chapter.)

Credibility. Generally, the individuals who have greatest expertise for assessing programmatic strengths and weaknesses—the faculty—are also the individuals whose self-interests are closely tied to the conclusions of the program review. State agency staffs understand these realities and, as a result, are constantly on the alert for a whitewash. Uncertainty about motives may lead the faculty to believe that all external parties are seeking evidence that would support program discontinuance. On the other hand, state agency staffs may view any data or conclusions developed by those directly responsible for the program with considerable skepticism; because of this, they may reject relevant information or fail to act on the basis of sound conclusions. So a conflict in objectives—involving expertise while maintaining trust and credibility—is always present. Too many program reviews have not resolved these conflicts and are consequently counterproductive. The chapters by Hoyt and by House discuss the ramifications of this issue.

Checks and Balances. A program review process is often organized around a complex mosaic of interlocking committees to establish checks and balances that simultaneously strengthen credibility and provide channels for consultation and information flow. Many campuses have established hierarchical committee structures involving the program faculty as well as faculty in other disciplines that have a reputation for academic leadership and understanding. From a state perspective, a program review would be well advised to understand these checks and balances, insist that they are workable and, hence, credible, and then build upon them. Even though some colleges and universities give considerable attention to establishing appropriate organizational structures to support a program review process, these efforts often fail because the responsibilities and reporting relationships of each group or committee are not clearly defined. Again, this lack of definition is often a subtle way of circumventing conflicts and tensions. In the end, however, this strategy will lead to even greater distrust.

External Consultants. External consultants offer an opportunity to replicate much of the expertise that is available through the program's faculty and, at the same time, external consultants are further detached from the ramifications of the recommendations that result from program review. Consequently, external consultants are likely to call the shots as they see them. But external consultants can add substantial costs to the program review process. Furthermore, the question of who commissions the consultants is a sensitive issue. For example, if a state agency selects or pays the consultants, they may well be viewed as "hired guns." If the program faculty selects the consultants, the review will be viewed as another "inside job." There are, of course, options between these extremes. For example, consultants can be commissioned by one party with the advice or consent of other parties. Such compromises can result in satisfactory choices from the perspective of all involved. An in-depth discussion of the pros and cons associated with the use of consultants in program review is presented by Petrie in Chapter Two.

Positive Incentives. Although it is not easy, creating positive incentives in a program review can be accomplished through such means as:

- Assurance of due process; the program review process does not always lead to positive conclusions from everyone's perspective, so it is important that all perspectives are heard and carefully considered.
- Building in the potential for tangible payoffs; a clean bill of health may be viewed as a nice result (given all the bad things that could have occurred), but a commitment to capitalize on what has been learned from a review, even though this may involve considerable expense, can be far more meaningful.
- Linkage to other decision-making processes; a program review can easily become a process unto itself, with no realizable outlets. In such instances there is little reason to take reviews seriously.

Determining What Decisions Will Be Made as a Result of Program Review

Sometimes the conclusions and recommendations resulting from program reviews are transmitted to state agencies without the endorsement of the governing board or top level administrative officials. This is often true at other administrative levels within the institution. When this occurs surely something is amiss. The program review is seen as a half-hearted response to some externally imposed mandate, the results are not deemed to be valid, or key decision makers are ignoring the recommendations—perhaps because they feel that they are unsound, or perhaps because they do not believe they are in a strong enough position to implement them. Underlying all these possibilities frequently is a failure to conceptualize how program review results are to be linked effectively to other established decision-making processes of the academic unit, the institution, or the state agency, in particular, decisions related to budgets, personnel, curriculum, and future programmatic directions.

These decisions are closely aligned with many of the purposes of program review outlined in Table 1. The difficulties that are often encountered in implementing program review recommendations are a result of never having clarified or achieved a consensus on the purposes of the program at the outset. A related explanation for the problem that many institutions and state agencies face in implementing the recommendations of program review is that two different casts of characters are involved in the review process and the formal decision-making structures for budget, planning, personnel, and curriculum. For example, academic units, institutions, and state agencies have well established protocols for their budget processes. It is very difficult for an independently conceptualized and managed program review process to be superimposed upon these established budget protocols.

Program review, a relative newcomer in most institutions and state agencies, is likely to be staffed as an add-on, rather than integrated into the more established functions and organizational structures. Program review processes will be successful to the extent that they are conceptualized and staffed within the established organizational structures at all levels of higher education.

References

Barak, R. J., and Berdahl, R. O. *State Level Academic Program Review in Higher Education.* Denver, Colo.: Education Commission of the States, 1978.

Chance, W. "State Level Program Review." In *Postsecondary Education Program Review.* Boulder, Colo.: Western Interstate Commission for Higher Education, 1980.

Craven, E. "Evaluating Program Performance." In P. Jedamus and M. W. Peterson (Eds.), *Improving Academic Management: A Handbook of Planning and Institutional Research.* San Francisco: Jossey-Bass, 1980.

Engdahl, L., and Barak, R. "Study of Academic Program Review." In *Postsecondary*

Education Program Review. Boulder, Colo.: Western Interstate Commission for Higher Education, 1980.

Groves, R. T. "Program Review in a Multi-Level State Governance System: The Case of Illinois." *Planning for Higher Education,* 1979, *8* (1), 1–9.

Robert A. Wallhaus is deputy director for academic and health affairs at the Illinois Board of Higher Education.

Assessing administrative performance must begin with explication of contextual factors and unique characteristics that constrain or enhance opportunities.

Evaluating Administrators

Donald P. Hoyt

The role of administrator in higher education appears to have evolved from that of the ancient Greek gods. To judge from objective descriptions, its chief elements are to serve simultaneously as a source of salvation, a target for hostility, and a focus for blame. Given these expectations, we should not be surprised that few successful administrators have been identified. As a group, they are subject to the same frustrations that Sam Levinson attributed to the children in his family. When unexpected callers arrived at dinner time, the quick-thinking Mother Levinson ordered the children to decline the chicken so that there would be enough for the guests. As the time came for the apple pie, the children understandably felt resentful when she announced that those who had not eaten their chicken would not be served dessert. With that ploy, Sam's mother served as one of our first experts in training administrators.

The double- and triple-binds that seem to be inherent in the role of administrator create a challenge to those concerned with evaluating these professionals. To ease into this challenge, I will review a few principles of personnel evaluation, which will then be applied to the task of evaluating administrators.

Principles of Evaluation

Numerous books have been written on evaluation principles and their implications for evaluation processes (see, for example, Antsey, Fletcher, and

R. Wilson (Ed.). *New Directions for Higher Education: Designing Academic Program Reviews,* no. 37.
San Francisco: Jossey-Bass, March 1982.

Walker, 1976 and Bolar, 1978). From this literature, those principles shown by experience to be essential to a successful program will be discussed. Most of these principles address multiple concerns but, for convenience, I have organized them around three criteria for a sound evaluation program — procedures should be credible, valid, and fair.

Regrettably, these characteristics are not always compatible. Therefore, actions taken to maximize one may detract from another. Practical experience suggests that credibility is the most vital; the concerned parties must have confidence that the procedures are appropriate and will yield meaningful results. Credibility is largely a political matter. Without a dependable base of political support, few programs can succeed.

Validity, on the other hand, is more of a technical matter. It refers to the comprehensiveness or completeness of evaluation processes and to the accuracy of the judgments that result from them. Although it would be unethical to employ procedures or tools known to be invalid, it may be necessary to choose the less valid of two procedures in order to improve credibility.

The final criterion of sound evaluation programs is that they be fair. In contrast to the political nature of credibility and the technical nature of validity, fairness represents a moral imperative. It insists that professional ethics be followed, that procedures be applied uniformly, and that objectivity be pursued.

Given this framework, let us review the chief principles that emerge from these criteria.

General Principles. Two principles are so fundamental that they support all three of the requirements of a sound evaluation program. These are the principles of *uniqueness* and *contextual interpretation.*

Uniqueness. Administrators must be evaluated on the basis of mutual understanding of a unique set of job expectations. If one were determined to dismiss a particular administrator, but feared that some law such as those guaranteeing civil rights or equal opportunity might be used to frustrate this desire, there is a sure way out: Don't tell the administrator what is expected, what he or she will be held accountable for. Because there is always more that needs doing than time to do it, there will be no difficulty in discovering matters that have been ignored or neglected. With no prior understanding of expectations, such "oversights" will provide objective and rational justification for even the most vindictive decisions.

Contextual Interpretation. When "student achievement" is used to judge teaching effectiveness, those whose classes are dominated by highly motivated, intellectually quick students have an unfair advantage over those whose students are slow and resistant to learning. Similarly, administrators should be evaluated within the context of the resources they had, the personal or situational obstructions they encountered, and other factors that affect outcomes but are beyond the administrator's control.

Principles Related to Fairness. Activities and enterprises lacking a sound moral base have destructive tendencies that ultimately result in their own demise. Therefore, it is appropriate to begin with a review of principles specifically related to fairness. Besides the generalized principles of uniqueness and contextual interpretation, fairness requires *openness* and *relevance.*

Openness. An evaluation is not the place for hidden cameras, no matter how much they might contribute to validity. Individuals asked to report their observations or to make evaluative judgments should be told why their reactions are being sought, what will be done with their input, and what the rules are governing the confidentiality of their reports. Similarly, the process should not be mysterious to the person being evaluated. Although a guarantee of confidentiality to those making observations relevant to evaluation is usually desirable, the fairness principle suggests that these remarks should not be made anonymously. There should be a valid way for a disinterested outsider to determine if the evaluator faithfully summarized confidential material from others.

Relevance. It would be unfair to fault a teacher of the retarded because none of her graduates had qualified as a national merit scholar. Similarly, it would be unfair to fault an administrator for low faculty salaries, poor faculty research productivity, or declining enrollments if her assignments were exclusively in areas unrelated to these disasters. Evaluative measures should bear a clear association to the responsibilities assigned to and accepted by the administrator.

Principles Related to Credibility. Two additional principles of evaluation are especially useful for ensuring credibility, the principles of *power* and *reinforcement.*

Power. The power principle states that, to be credible, evaluation procedures should be developed with input from all affected parties. One reason that highly similar student evaluation systems have blossomed on hundreds of campuses is that, unless those affected have their say, the procedures will always be regarded as insensitive to the local situation. Sometimes it is necessary to reinvent the wheel.

Although the individuals or groups being evaluated clearly are entitled to provide advice, they are not the only interested parties. This is particularly true of administrators whose work is of concern to students, subordinates, colleagues, and superiors, including the governing board. An evaluation system that denies any of these constituencies an opportunity to reveal their biases runs a serious credibility risk.

The principle does not require that all advice be accepted. It does require that opinions be sought and that a rationale be formulated to engender belief that the system was aware of the perspective of each group.

Reinforcement. The second principle related to credibility—reinforcement—states that the acceptability of evaluation procedures is a function of their potential for positive effects. This principle is derived from the obvious fact that evaluation is inherently threatening. People have been programmed to focus on its negative effects, partly because whenever a shake-up is desired, it is traditional to call for an evaluative review. More fundamentally, evaluation is a judgmental process; the worth of a person or program is presumably being determined. For the rare person whose high ego strength and self-confidence are justified by competence and accomplishment, evaluation may be a neutral, or even welcome, activity. But for the vast majority who harbor some self-doubts, who are aware of some personal weaknesses, and who desire and need the support and confidence of others, evaluation poses the distinct prospect that they will be found out.

Therefore, the evaluation system should feature the potential for gain. That is, if it discovers something amiss, it should provide some mechanism for righting it. This correction may mean improving administrative skills; it may also mean increasing resources, altering priorities, or reorganizing an administrative unit.

Principles Related to Validity. Two components determine the validity of evaluations—comprehensiveness and accuracy. Principles related to validity, including the generalized principles of uniqueness and contextual interpretation, stress one or the other of these components.

Criterion Specification. One of the major mistakes made by evaluation neophytes is the confusion of "description" with "evaluation." A description of activities is different from a judgment of their impact. To know what happened as a result of the administrator's activities is much more important than whether he worked hard, was on time, or called people by their first names.

The principle requires that a description of relevant outcomes be prepared for each of the major activities identified with a position. Valid evaluation procedures will specify the changes in people, situations, or accomplishments that differentiate the successful from the unsuccessful administrator. The process of identifying relevant criteria will also require specifying appropriate time frames. Some outcomes will be observable only after several years, while others are relatively continuous.

Face Value of Evidence. A second principle related to validity requires that evidence used for appraisal have an obvious relationship to the criteria that are selected. The relevance of each piece of evaluative information should be undisputed.

Many programs using student ratings of instruction to evaluate teaching effectiveness fail because they ask students to make judgments for which they are unqualified (the teacher's knowledge of the material) or ratings of characteristics whose relevance to teaching effectiveness was dubious (sense of humor, for example). Administrative evaluation programs can fail for similar reasons. Faculty are ill-equipped to rate such a statement as "effectiveness with which the dean represents the college to other deans." And the consequences of characteristics like "hard-headedness" or "soft-heartedness" have not been nearly so well established as have the biases of their champions.

Representativeness of Input. One of the most serious affronts to the dignity of a "true-blue" evaluator is the letter of recommendation. Finding someone who will cleverly disguise the truth or who is unaware of it is not difficult. But little can be learned from such unrepresentative sources, even if honesty could be assured. Little of value is gained when a visitor registers an unsolicited complaint about the person being evaluated.

Given the shaky reliability and validity of the observations of any one individual, it is vital that steps be taken to ensure that judgments from a given source are representative of that source. If the number of potential observers is high, a procedure for sampling them at random is preferable to input from a larger, self-selected number.

Another aspect of representativeness is especially important in the evaluation of administrators. Where feasible, ratings of the same characteristics should be obtained from multiple sources. Since deans typically deal with vice-presidents, other deans, department chairman, and faculty, each of these groups has observed behaviors related to a characteristic like integrity. If they agree, confidence in the evaluation is increased, since both circumstances and raters were representative.

The Responsibilities of the Administrator

The preceding brief review of principles should make it obvious that the evaluation process must begin with the specification of expectations. For what responsibilities will the administrator be held accountable? The list ought to be different for every administrator and every setting, for it should reflect unique histories and the idiosyncratic nature of local circumstances, including the capabilities and quirks of the local cast of characters.

Although uniqueness must be preserved, an outline can offer suggestions from which particular responsibilities may be chosen and given priorities appropriate to the local situation. For this purpose administrative activities may be grouped into four major foci—those concerned with planning, image building, decision making, and evaluation.

1. *Planning Activities.* Activities classified as planning include the following: explicating objectives for the unit, establishing priorities, developing ways to address priorities, and creating an organization scheme that facilitates implementation of these plans. A serious, but common, administrative mistake is to implement and nourish programs or activities directed to the wrong concerns. A parallel error in evaluating administrators is to focus evaluative attention on how well current activities are being conducted without attending to the prior question of whether they should be conducted at all.

2. *Image-building Activities.* This category includes efforts to improve the climate needed to support the unit's work. Some of these are internal, relating to policies, practices, and communication mechanisms that promote or detract from a climate of good will and dedication among members of the unit. Others are external, including those concerned with building external support for the

unit (among other units, higher level administrators, constituencies such as governing boards and patrons) and those concerned with obtaining resources needed to address priorities successfully.

3. *Decision-making Activities.* In this category are decisions involving resource allocation and the acquisition of personnel or environmental support (facilities, equipment) needed to accomplish the unit's objectives. All kinds of decisions are made on a daily basis, but those that determine who will do the work and what resources they will have are the most critical.

4. *Evaluation Activities.* Administrators are often charged with responsibilities for evaluating both the personnel who report to them and the programs conducted under the administrator's authority. They may also have responsibility for monitoring the evaluation activities conducted by their subordinates.

From this list of activities, a list of expectations appropriate to a given administrator at a given time can be developed. The explication of such a list is needed to meet the generalized principle of uniqueness. Contextual interpretation, the other generalized principle, is considered in the next section.

Contextual Factors

The number of factors that may represent extenuating circumstances is nearly limitless. A valid, credible, and fair evaluation of the administrator's effectiveness will require understanding and interpreting factors such as the following.

1. *History and Tradition.* What environmental supports or obstacles have an impact on the administrator's efforts? For example, if planning is a new activity to the institution or unit, initial expectations should be modest. If there are serious schisms among members of the unit—young versus old, tenured versus nontenured, researchers versus teachers, and so on—the tasks for the administrator assume special difficulties that require the attenuation of expectations. If the unit's personnel have been fairly stable over the past few years and are generally regarded as competent professionals, expectations of the administrator should be considerably greater than when the opposite is true. To establish "standards" for acceptable performance of administrative responsibilities is unreasonable unless one is aware of historical forces that facilitate or impede the achievement of objectives.

2. *Availability of Resources.* History does not record a single instance in which administrative leaders of an institution or unit felt that resources were adequate. Clearly, poverty is a relative matter (Bowen, 1980). Although it is tempting to excuse or explain all disappointing outcomes on the basis of inadequate resources, this is most clearly justified when outcomes are directly tied to resource limitations. For example, a goal of improving the research capabilities of the faculty is likely to be frustrated if salary schedules are not competitive with those at research institutions. Similarly, when reviewers emphasize the lack of equipment or computing facilities as a major reason for disapprov-

ing an extramural proposal, one is justified in inferring that resource limitations were important factors in the administrator's failure to attract outside funds.

3. *Self-government Expectations.* The task of the administrator is seriously altered to the degree that the unit's personnel are committed to the ideal of self-government. There are instances where faculty members want nothing more than to be left alone to do their jobs; they expect administrative support and a minimum of distraction. In other units, every move of an administrator is second-guessed and an action taken without complete consultation with all concerned becomes fodder for paranoia and hostility.

4. *The Visibility of Alternative Models.* Administrative style or procedures may be conditioned by the availability and visibility of alternative models. For example, stimulating the submission of grant proposals may be difficult to achieve if some members of the unit make highly disparaging comparisons between the institution's policy regarding overhead funds and that at other institutions. Similarly, department heads may find it difficult to implement their administrative roles with faculty accustomed to and supportive of the chairperson system. An awareness that faculty members in some universities are full partners in the budgetary allocation process may make it difficult to conduct the process under less democratic arrangements, even if these are mandated by trustees.

5. *Chance.* Unpredictable circumstances that affect administrative effectiveness will almost certainly arise. The administrator who suffers a heart attack and spends six months on sick leave will almost surely be unable to accomplish his objectives for the year. Administrators of state-supported institutions will be unable to meet many objectives if they are required to institute sizable unscheduled budget reductions due to overestimations of available tax revenues. An epidemic of violent assaults and other crimes on campus can easily disrupt an administrator's plans, activities, and time schedule.

Collecting Evaluative Information

An effective evaluation system begins with a description of the responsibilities to be emphasized during the evaluation period. It ends with an interpretation of evaluation information based on performance standards and an understanding of contextual factors. Between these two points evaluative information is collected.

Two types of evaluative information are needed. One has to do with outcomes: What evidence is there that desired changes have occurred as a result of the administrator's activities? The second concerns administrative style: How can this administrator's approach be characterized? The first of these is needed for *summative* evaluation, a judgment of effectiveness used to make personnel recommendations. Information regarding style is relevant to *formative* evaluation, whose purpose is to understand why effectiveness was high or low so that improvement suggestions can be made (Bloom, Hastings, and Madaus, 1971).

In designing the process for collecting evaluative information, two questions must be answered. What information is needed? How can it be obtained? Once there is an understanding on the relative emphasis to be given to planning, decision making, evaluating, and public relations activities, the types of outcomes expected must be made explicit in the form of observable products or impressions of others.

Begin with a list of expected products. If planning responsibilities are stressed, one or more plans should be developed. Memoranda or formal papers that describe these plans, objectives, and priorities are examples of products. Formal program reviews or personnel evaluations are illustrative of the products expected from evaluative responsibilities. Similarly, the acquisition of resources and equipment and the credentials of personnel are products that directly reflect at least some aspects of image promotion and decision making.

The existence of such products is seldom sufficient for evaluation. Plans, objectives, and priorities differ in quality, appropriateness, and timeliness; those that are inferior on these dimensions may be worse than none. The same is true of most other products; some mechanism is needed for inferring how well the product responds to the need.

This raises the question of who should judge these products. The answer is those who are qualified and willing. Regrettably, such individuals or groups usually make their judgments from a limited frame of reference. The departmental faculty can render a useful judgment about the appropriateness of a projected plan for accomplishing objectives. But their frame of reference for making this judgment may be quite different from that of the vice-president whose perception of the department's role may differ drastically from the faculty's view.

Three rules, if followed, will improve the usefulness of such ratings. First, do not ask for ratings if there are serious doubts about the rater's qualifications to supply useful information. Second, seek ratings from several individuals of similar status to compensate for differences in personalities or preferences. Third, obtain judgments from diverse sources so that a comprehensive perspective is provided.

The preceding discussion focused on the rating of products. A second type of outcome concerns criteria related to atmosphere or attitudes. Administrators are often charged with the responsibility of promoting faculty morale, increasing cooperation within the unit and with other units, and establishing a positive work environment. Such objectives seldom have products that can be judged for their impact, although the development of policy statements or the establishment of communication mechanisms are obvious exceptions. Attitudinal outcomes are usually best described by those to whom the objectives are directed. Thus, the assessment of morale and related characteristics requires a direct inquiry of individuals in the work setting.

Although ratings of products and of attitudinal outcomes are needed for summative evaluation, they will seldom serve formative purposes. Improvement strategies require evaluative information about administrative style, the ways and means by which administrative responsibilities are executed.

Several frameworks have been suggested for describing styles. One of these is derived from empirical analyses of department needs (Hoyt and Spangler, 1978, 1979). It specifies four relatively independent dimensions of style. The first dimension emphasizes "democratic practice"; individuals in the unit are consulted on nearly every decision, and their collective preference is used as a guide to policy or decision making. A second is labelled "structuring"; the emphasis is on establishing a strict set of policies, procedures, and expectations that are established and adhered to in a highly predictable way. The third dimension, "interpersonal sensitivity," is largely a human relations factor; here the impact of the administrator and administrative actions on the personal life of individuals is emphasized. "Vigor" is the final dimension; administrators who are high on this characteristic are perceived as ambitious and energetic stimulants.

The scheme used to describe administrative style is less important than the reason for making the effort. The primary rationale is to uncover potential explanations for disappointing ratings of effectiveness. Style serves to facilitate or inhibit the achievement of objectives. Preliminary data suggest that different styles may be needed for different objectives. Thus, in the studies by Hoyt and Spangler, faculty morale was highest in departments in which the dominant administrative style included democratic practice and interpersonal sensitivity. In contrast, administrators who were most successful in communicating the department's needs for resources had administrative styles that emphasized structuring and vigor.

Conclusions and Implications

From the foregoing analyses, several conclusions can be suggested. First, a thorough evaluation of any administrator requires a highly individualistic design that is sensitive to idiosyncracies in the history and current status of the unit to be administered. Although it may help to examine models, procedures, and instruments that have been employed elsewhere, applying these to different situations creates a procrustean bed that tortures both its occupant and those who are his neighbors. For these reasons, normative judgments, such as "average" and "above average," are usually inappropriate. Administrator evaluation will almost always require criterion referenced measures; in brief, whether or not a given level of performance is satisfactory must be determined by preestablished expectations, or standards, not by a percentile rank.

Second, evaluation of administrators is unusually complex. This is true for a variety of reasons. Most administrators have multiple constituencies;

lines of communication and influence go up, down, and sideways. Fellow administrators on the same level (fellow deans, department heads, presidents of institutions in a system) interact about matters that differ from those shared by the administrator and subordinates or by the administrator and superiors. Therefore, although several individuals can provide competent observations of administrative styles and their outcomes, none has the opportunity to perceive the entire arena. Understandably, conflicting reports are not uncommon, and they may all be correct. Multiple sources of evaluative judgment should be sought, judgments should be confined to those for which the rater is qualified by experience and by opportunity to observe, and reconciliation of all evaluative input may be impossible.

Aside from differences arising from the perspectives and roles of the various constituencies, evaluation is complicated by contextual matters. The sound evaluator will recognize that most measures of administrative effectiveness represent multiple variables, only one of which is administrative behavior. Conclusions regarding administrative effectiveness require a sensitive understanding of the complexities of the situation, seasoned insight into the presence and importance of extraneous circumstances, and integrity and wisdom in drawing conclusions about the portion of outcome variance which can properly be attributed to the administrator.

Third, many important outcomes of administrative behavior cannot be immediately observed. Full implementation of substantive plans frequently requires several years. Outcomes of specific programs or policies cannot always be judged by their immediate effects. The honeymoon for a new administrator may have a temporary positive impact on morale or environment which is not indicative of enduring effects.

These observations suggest two additional implications. First, an essential ingredient for the evaluation of administrators is a comprehensive annual report that reviews objectives, priorities, activities, and outcomes; other inputs are also needed, but the annual report provides the administrator with an opportunity to display skills related to planning, decision making, and evaluation. Such a report also allows an administrator to identify factors that affect the interpretation of outcomes. Second, a comprehensive evaluation can be undertaken only every three to five years. Even football coaches are usually given enough time to demonstrate the effects of their recruitment, retention, and coaching efforts.

Finally, for humane, economic, and political reasons, administrative evaluation should not be undertaken without a commitment to using it for improvement. On the humane side, individuals deserve an opportunity to learn from their mistakes. Economically, improvements in administrative effectiveness may result in increased efficiency and reduced costs. Politically, it is desirable to avoid the pattern established by politicians of launching their reelection campaign the day after the polls close. The reappointment of academic administrators ought to depend more on their success in identifying and correcting weaknesses than on their skill in hiding these weaknesses from their constituents.

This consideration indicates that a provision be made for providing relatively continuous evaluative feedback that can be used for diagnostic purposes. Expert consultation should be employed to assist administrators in developing improvement strategies, and some resources should be made available to implement them.

These conclusions can be summarized in the form of a plan for administrative evaluation:

1. Administrative appointments should be for fixed periods, generally three to five years.
2. The appointment period should begin with a statement of goals, objectives, and priorities for the coming year and the next few years and end with a review of progress on these, the circumstances that altered plans or affected outcomes, and a projection for the next cycle.
3. The evaluation process, which requires relevant input from a variety of sources, should be conducted by a special committee whose members are respected representatives of each constituency. An authority in evaluation should lead the committee and, in the case of high-level administrators, might well include an advocate for the administrator—a person who understands the circumstances under which the administrator functioned and who deliberately attempts to interpret evaluative information in the best light. The chairman should see that sound principles of evaluation are followed (see Hoyt, 1974).
4. At the conclusion of the evaluation, a decision should be made about reappointment. If this decision is affirmative, plans should be made to address professional development and program improvement needs identified by the evaluation.
5. A provision should also be made to obtain less-comprehensive evaluative input on an annual basis. Such input should be secured on a volunteer and confidential basis, and its purpose should be limited to diagnosis for developing improvement strategies (Office of Educational Resources, 1978).

References

Anstey, E., Fletcher, C., and Walker, J. *Staff Appraisal and Development.* London: Allen and Unwin, 1976.

Bloom, B. S., Hastings, J. T., and Madaus, G. F. *Handbook on Formative and Summative Evaluation.* New York: McGraw-Hill, 1971.

Bolar, M. (Ed.). *Performance Appraisal: Readings, Case Studies, and a Survey of Practices.* New Delhi: Vikas, 1978.

Bowen, H. R. *The Costs of Higher Education: How Much Do Colleges and Universities Spend per Student and How Much Should They Spend?* San Francisco: Jossey-Bass, 1980.

Hoyt, D. P. *Guidelines for the Evaluation of Academic Deans.* Manhattan: Kansas State University, 1974 (Mimeograph).

Hoyt, D. P., and Spangler, R. K. "Administrative Effectiveness of the Academic Department Head: Correlates of Effectiveness." *Research Report No. 47.* Manhattan: Office of Educational Resources, Kansas State University, 1978.

Hoyt, D. P., and Spangler, R. K. "The Measurement of Administrative Effectiveness of the Academic Department Head." *Research in Higher Education*, 1979, *10,* 291–304.

Office of Educational Resources. *Faculty Reactions to the Academic Dean.* Manhattan: Kansas State University, 1978.

Donald P. Hoyt is assistant vice-president of academic affairs and director of the Office of Educational Resources at Kansas State University.

Those responsible for monitoring evaluation systems should be aware of contributions that not only are immediate and observable but also are delayed, unintended, and obscured.

Concluding Statement and Additional Readings

Richard F. Wilson

As stated at the outset, this sourcebook was developed with special attention to documenting what has been learned about program evaluation in higher education and what important challenges remain. Evaluation is not an exact science, and conclusions are thus tentative. However, by virture of their prominence, several concepts and themes in the preceding chapters appear to be fundamental to program evaluation in higher education.

First, regardless of the general strategy employed, evaluation is value laden, and the more explicit we can be about the value positions of the audiences involved, the more likely we are to establish credible processes and produce informed results. Every step in evaluation requires that decisions be made, and decision alternatives should be examined in terms of the values being endorsed. The identification of evaluation purposes, criteria, data indicators, communication strategies, and reporting procedures have value implications to the same extent as evaluative conclusions and recommendations. Messages about values are being sent throughout the process, and lack of attention to the consistency of these messages may, at a minimum, confuse and perhaps even reinforce dysfunctional behavior.

Second, evaluations must be fair. The concept of fairness can be extended to include such things as validity, reliability, relevance, and openness. The quickest way to undermine conclusions, even correct ones, is to pro-

R. Wilson (Ed.). *New Directions for Higher Education: Designing Academic Program Reviews,* no. 37. San Francisco: Jossey-Bass, March 1982.

vide an opportunity for the process to be attacked as unfair. Three ways to limit such attacks is to spend considerable time developing and utilizing communication channels with relevant constituencies, to rely on multiple data sources in making evaluative judgments, and to instill flexibility and adaptiveness as basic organizing themes.

Finally, the number of approaches to evaluation described and advocated in this volume suggests that an ideal has yet to emerge that is equally applicable to all situations. The strategies mentioned—adaptive, responsive, systems analysis, behavioral, professional review, and case study—as well as those not mentioned—goal-based, goal-free, illuminative, decision-oriented, and juried—all make unique contributions that must be considered in light of institutional needs and resources. Practically, the strategy followed will likely be a hybrid, one established in response to local conditions rather than in accordance with a prescribed design.

Special Challenges

The unresolved issues and lingering problems that form the future agenda for evaluators are substantial, but four have been identified for special attention. The first has to do with the way we think about and measure quality. The resource constraints that currently exist and are expected for the future have made it critically important for institutions to document and protect areas of strength. It is important that effort continue to be expended in search of better measures of quality, measures that provide evidence of the significance, as opposed to the quantity, of work. There is, however, an important reality that should both inform and define expectations for such inquiries: Quality is an instrinsic attribute that may be inferred but never precisely determined. A judgment, albeit one fraught with value predispositions, is required to transform a series of quality measures into a decision about the attribute of quality itself.

A second challenge for evaluators in higher education, especially those of us who have given considerable attention to academic programs, is to begin developing methodologies that can be applied to nonacademic units. Faculty members who claim that program evaluation in higher education has been too narrowly focused cannot be rebuffed. Few institutions have developed anything close to a systematic procedure for evaluating administrative and support units. Part of the excuse is that such units are so dissimilar that a unique design must be established for every evaluation. Although a constraint, the inactivity in this area cannot continue. Beyond the obvious fact that administrative and service units receive significant budgetary support and therefore must be held accountable for the wise use of these funds, it is becoming increasingly clear that institutions with severe budget problems plan to protect academic units as long as possible. When institutions exhaust traditional budget-cutting options—deferred maintenance, across the board cuts, and reduced secretarial staff, for example—administrative and service units will be among the first to be scrutinized. Not only will these reviews be done, but they will be done quickly. Evaluators must develop expertise in conducting reviews of this type.

Another challenge for evaluators is to respond to institutional needs that cut across programs. Although current evaluation efforts may focus on degree offerings or departments, evaluation processes must be established with sufficient flexibility so that special institutional concerns that relate to more than one program can be explored. Examples would include the quality of instruction provided by teaching assistants, course duplication, and continuing education contributions.

Finally, evaluators must ensure that procedures are established to monitor what is being accomplished. Is the evaluation system performing in a satisfactory way? What purposes are being achieved? What evidence exists to suggest that the institution and its units are benefitting from evaluation? These are a few of the questions which should be addressed on a regular basis. This monitoring activity should involve evaluators but not be undertaken by them. Those responsible for the task should be alerted to the importance of judging a system not only on the basis of the immediate and the observable but also on the basis of the delayed, the unintended, and the obscured. As evaluators, we, more than anyone else, must not be guilty of perpetuating poor performance. We must seek continuing advice on whether our work is making a positive contribution.

Additional Readings

The evaluation references that follow are arranged topically and were selected to provide an orientation to the field of evaluation generally and to program evaluation in higher education specifically.

General References

Anderson, S. B., and Ball, S. *The Profession and Practice of Program Evaluation.* San Francisco: Jossey-Bass, 1978.

Caro, F. G. *Readings in Evaluation Research.* New York: Russell Sage Foundation, 1977.

Cronbach, L. J., and others. *Toward Reform of Program Evaluation: Aims, Methods, and Institutional Arrangements.* San Francisco: Jossey-Bass, 1980.

Rose, C., and Nyre, G. F. *The Practice of Evaluation.* ERIC/TM Report No. 65. Princeton, N.J.: ERIC Clearinghouse on Tests, Measurement, and Evaluation, 1977.

Weiss, C. H. *Evaluating Action Programs: Readings in Social Action and Organization.* Boston: Allyn & Bacon, 1972.

Evaluation Approaches

Campbell, D. T., and Stanley, J. C. *Experimental and Quasi-Experimental Designs for Research.* Chicago: Rand-McNally, 1963.

Parlett, M., and Dearden, G. (Eds.). *Introduction to Illuminative Evaluation: Studies in Higher Education.* Berkeley, Calif.: Pacific Soundings Press, 1977.

Provus, N. *Discrepancy Evaluation for Educational Program Improvement and Assessment.* Berkeley, Calif.: McCutchan, 1971.

Rippey, R. M. (Ed.). *Studies in Transactional Evaluation.* Berkeley, Calif.: McCutchan, 1973.

Scriven, M. "Goal-Free Evaluation." In E. R. House (Ed.), *School Evaluation: The Politics and Process.* Berkeley, Calif.: McCutchan, 1973.

Stake, R. E. *Program Evaluation, Particularly Responsive Evaluation.* Paper No. 5 in Occasional Paper Series. Kalamazoo: Evaluation Center, Western Michigan University, November 1975.

Stufflebeam, D. L., and others. *Educational Evaluation and Decision Making.* Itasca, Ill.: Peacock, 1971.

Suchman, E. A. *Evaluative Research.* New York: Russell Sage Foundation, 1967.

Evaluation Issues

Braskamp, L. A., and Brown, R. D. (Eds.). *New Directions for Program Evaluation: Utilization of Evaluative Information,* no. 5. San Francisco: Jossey-Bass, 1980.

Guttentag, M. "Subjectivity and Its Use in Evaluation Research." *Evaluation,* 1973, *1* (2), 60–65.

House, E. R. *The Politics of Educational Innovation.* Berkeley, Calif.: McCutchan, 1974.

Lawrence, J. K., and Green, K. C. *The Higher Education Rating Game: A Question of Quality.* An ERIC/Higher Education Research Report. Washington, D.C.: American Association for Higher Education, 1980.

Olscamp, P. J. "Can Program Quality Be Quantified?" *Journal of Higher Education,* 1978, *49* (5), 504–511.

Patton, M. Q. *Utilization Focused Evaluation.* Beverly Hills, Calif.: Sage, 1978.

Evaluation in Higher Education

Barak, R. J., and Berdahl, R. O. *State Level Academic Program Review in Higher Education.* Denver, Colo.: Education Commission of the States, 1978.

Craven, E. C. (Ed.). *New Directions for Institutional Research: Alternative Models of Academic Program Evaluation,* no. 27. San Francisco: Jossey-Bass, 1980.

Dressel, P. L. *Handbook for Academic Evaluation: Assessing Institutional Effectiveness, Student Progress, and Professional Performance for Decision Making in Higher Education.* San Francisco: Jossey-Bass, 1976.

Folger, J. K. (Ed.). *New Directions for Institutional Research: Increasing the Public Accountability of Higher Education,* no. 16. San Francisco: Jossey-Bass, 1977.

Green, K. C. "Program Review and the State Responsibility for Higher Education." *Journal of Higher Ecucation,* 1981, *52* (1), 67–80.

Administrator Evaluation

Farmer, C. H. *Administrator Evaluation: Concepts, Methods, Cases in Higher Education.* Richmond, Va.: Higher Education Leadership and Management Society, 1979.

Fisher, C. F. (Ed.). *New Directions for Higher Education: Developing and Evaluating Administrative Leadership,* no. 22. San Francisco: Jossey-Bass, 1978.

Goodwin, H. I., and Smith, E. R. *Faculty and Administrator Evaluation: Constructing the Instruments.* Morgantown, W. Va.: College of Human Resources and Education, West Virginia University, 1981.

Munitz, B. "Examining Administrative Performance." In P. Jedamus, M. W. Peterson, and Associates (Eds.), *Improving Academic Management: A Handbook of Planning and Institutional Research.* San Francisco: Jossey-Bass, 1980.

Richard F. Wilson is assistant vice-chancellor for academic affairs and assistant professor of higher education at the University of Illinois at Urbana-Champaign.

Index

E

F

G

H

I

K

L

M

N

O

P

Q

R

S

T

U

V

W

Y